Our Public Schools:
A Pearl of Great Price

Frank Schneider, ED.D.

Factor Press
P.O. Box **8888**
Mobile, AL **36689**

2000

ISBN: 1-887650-19-9

Publisher's Cataloging In Publication
Schneider, Frank.
    Our public schools: a pearl of great price/Frank Schneider.

    p. cm.

    ISBN 1-887650-19-9

    1. Public schools—United States. 2. Educational change—United States. 3. Education—United States—Aims and objectives. 4. Teachers—United States—Evaluation. I. Title
    LA 217.S3 200

Cover art by Teresa Mathews
Typeset by Ronald E. Feuerlein

CONTENTS

PART FIVE
DEBILITATING INFLUENCES............................61

PART SIX
LEGAL, REGULATORY, AND
    ADMINISTRATIVE BASES FOR
    RENEWAL...121

FOREWORD

Battles have been fought over public education throughout the history of America, but we have never been as close as now to the demise of our system of state public schools.

The American public school system is fighting a war on two fronts for its very existence. On one front, the federal government seeks to nationalize public education. On the other, the movement to privatize public schools supported by public tax monies is gaining momentum.

Since World War II, our schools have increasingly failed to meet our highest expectations. They have not evolved and renewed themselves, as all institutions must if they are to survive. Admittedly, the renewal process has not been ongoing within the school establishment, but, in addition, a host of deteriorative influences from without have left our schools incapable of carrying out their vital, traditional mission.

Public despair abounds. Citizens feel helpless. They no longer believe they have control of their children's education, and are unwilling to pay higher taxes for schools in which they have lost confidence. The purpose here is not to "heap on more coals." We are painfully aware of shortcomings and consequences of a failed educational system. We share the disappointment and frustration over the impending demise of our

Nation's most important institution, because of implementation of well-meaning, but short-sighted, inappropriate and politically motivated solutions. Our system of public schools has traditionally been considered "The Cornerstone of the American Republic" Because our representative democracy can be maintained only by a literate populace—a totally literate populace.

There is widespread belief that we cannot salvage our schools and they should be abandoned. The movement to choose alternative schools may grow and succeed, and may eventually operate as private and parochial schools now do, but funded with public tax monies.

The sharp decline in educational performance was noted in the 1960s, not only on the basis of test results, but the acute awareness of teachers, college professors, and dismayed employers who found the end product seriously lacking. No condemnation of the prevailing condition of our schools was more searing than that expressed by Edgar B. Wesley in the following statement, which he titled, "The Criticis Creed":

> I believe in the failure of American education, in the superiority of foreign schools, the inferiority of American teachers, the frivolity of our curriculum, the superficiality of education requirements, and the degradation of teacher training.
>
> ...I renounce the doctrines of motivation, progressiveness, life-adjustment, permissiveness, and the whole child. In contrast to these delusions I assert my faith in discipline, drill, the transfer of training, phonetics, the segregation of the gifted, and the power of positive teaching. Educational salvation for America can be achieved by abandoning social, emotional, artistic, physical, and vocational aims, by concentrating upon mental development, and by chanting

incessantly the wonder-working phrases "basic education," "higher standards," and "excellence."

What Wesley believes needs to be done is what most Americans also believe. It will not be easy to accomplish, but power is actually available for American citizens,to put in place school reforms that are needed.

The chapters that follow are not intended to address the myriad of issues about public education; rather, only a selected few aspects are discussed because of their immediate, influence on teachers and what happens in classrooms. Several chapters are included because they are written about in popular media (which tend to misdirect and cloud our vision as we seek to revitalize and renew our schools).

There may not be wide agreement with the beliefs and recommendations that follow. I intend them to serve only as schematics in a reconstruction process. Working drawings need to be made by the several bodies that converge to make public education possible. Not the least hope is that the material will provoke study and discussion and reaffirm that our public schools are, indeed, a "Pearl of Great Price."

Part I   reminds us of the need to set goals and objectives in keeping with the vision we have for public education in America.

Part II   presents belief statements that should be regarded as foundational for any effort to renew our schools-beliefs that have been increasingly disregarded.

Part III focuses on teachers, each of whom represents the entire system of public education in a given class room. The demise of public education will not be prevented until schools are staffed entirely with competent teachers.

Part IV identifies two movements currently gaining acceptance that pose an imminent threat to public education.

Part V is a series of essays, or "reflections," on selected topics and practices that are believed to be debilitating influences.

Part VI points to legal power of elected and appointed officials that should be marshaled to achieve school reform.

Part VII is a plea for the sacrificial effort we must make, and a warning if we do not.

PART ONE

Vision for Hope and Renewal

CHAPTER 1

Charting a New Direction

The fervent hope of parents in all cultures has been for their children to be well trained, and educated, and to become healthy, moral, and fully functioning adults. All developed countries rely on some kind for formal system of education to accomplish such objectives.

Our public schools have served us well. They have played a decisive role in the development of a single nation, in bringing millions of immigrants into full participation in American life, in preserving and strengthening the democratic system of government, in facilitating widespread social mobility, and in promoting economic growth and prosperity[1]

Not strongly felt, however, were foreboding changes that began after World War II, apparently masked by overall prosperity and the hustle and bustle of people working to reestablish their lives. The most resounding alarm was heard in the news of the Russian accomplishments in math and science, followed by countless reports critical of our public schools. By 1960, we acknowledged that we simply had stopped doing the right things. Traditional educational practices were discarded, expectations were lowered, and the curriculum was "dumbed down."[2]

Efforts to improve our schools have always been on-going, but so-called reform movements have never been more varied and diverse, or intense, since 1970. Unfortunately, most of the reforms have proven worthless and even counterproductive. They have been imposed from the "top down," beyond the control of those inside the educational establishment, and those who work directly with children.

William Gardner blames the "State, for causing collectivist results; runaway costs per student; an empire of academic bureaucrats; mediocre academic performance; a suppression of the core values of a free society; and hoards of overweight, unfit children. He recommends that citizens "take back their schools."[3]

An echo of that motif is heard throughout this book. We should not forget the warning that any institution that does not continually evolve and renew itself is doomed to deteriorate and perish. We should have faith that our schools were actually on an evolving path—perhaps, too slowly—but, to a proper destination. Desperate and foolhardy reform measures caused a detour to a path we should not have taken. (The "fork in the road" metaphor is referred to in Chapter 31.) It is to be hoped that we will return to the point where we took a wrong turn.

Our public schools are blessed with many outstanding teachers and administrators who work diligently and selflessly for our children. They carry on despite conditions and influences that they believe affect the quality of the schools and, eventually, the decline in the quality of life in our country. In light of the environment in which our schools now operate, improvement may not come about without powerful, broad-front interdiction.

Our schools did not deteriorate overnight. We should not expect them to be corrected overnight. Nevertheless, we should begin, but only from a base of sound principles that we should have learned from history. If what is set forth here only provides worthwhile material for study, examination, and incorporation in future planning, it will have served its purpose.

PART TWO

Foundational Beliefs

CHAPTER 2

Public Education Is Essential

The purpose of the American public school system, the oldest in the world, in its broadest sense, is to prepare children and youth for citizenship in our representative democracy, also the oldest in the world. This purpose, central and unchanging, fits snugly in the framework of four, not mutually exclusive, broad educational goals that provide for:

- National security
- Intellectual development
- Perpetuation of our culture
- Citizenship in American Representative Democracy

Jefferson's timeless admonition, "A nation that expects to be ignorant and free, expects something that never was and never shall be," rings a continuing warning. Democracy will not work without a literate populace.

Man's survival on earth must be credited to education. Man, through observation, adaptation and trial and error, has with each succeeding generation empowered himself to control his destiny. Early education focused on survival skills with the family providing nurture and instruction in developing hunting skills, gathering and growing food, and training for defense and worship. Over time, purposes of education increased and became more diverse and specialized to reflect unique aims of various cultures that developed around the world. Our history traces from the time barbarians emerged from their primitive state through the development of Aryan, Sumerian, Semitic, and Hamitic cultures. This accumulated knowledge passed from generation to generation.

Around 1860, Herbert Spenser expressed a belief in two basic sources of knowledge: that which we gain as we live, and that which we inherit, including intuition. He identified major concerns of people, and these evolved as objectives of education in America. Those objectives included reading, writing, computing, health, worthy home membership, vocational competence, effective citizenship, and development of ethical character. This body of objectives is consistently included in reports that public schools submit to earn state and regional accreditation. These Cardinal Principles have stood the test of time despite 70 years of debate between utilitarian and liberal educators.

Education during our colonial era might be likened to a period of gestation leading to the birth of our nation in 1776. The formulation of our Constitution and Bill of Rights then shaped the framework for the realization of man's long search for individual freedom, the essential ingredient for human progress. Although we are not created physically or intellectually equal, we are entitled to equal opportunity for optimum development. Public school education, open to all children, makes this possible.

The body of our world's knowledge is doubling exponentially. The highest intellect is needed in every area of American life, including government, military, law, business, manufacturing, medicine, religion, and education.

Our public schools have heretofore served well to achieve educational goals and as the primary agency in shaping and maintaining a unified, socially cohesive nation. Generations of immigrants have merged their varied backgrounds into a naturalization process that assimilates customs, language, ideals, and values into the society we characterize as American. We take pride in the role of our schools to make this possible. Over the past 200 years American society has been marked by extensive, continuous change, and of all social institutions that have responded to the evolving demands and expectations of each successive generation, it has been our schools that have discharged those functions with amazing success.[1]

Ralph Tyler maintains that the United States could not have become the economic, military, and political giant that it has been except for the great contributions of the schools. They have provided a labor force, helped millions of immigrants to adapt to their new land, prepared individuals for leadership roles, and reinforced the concept of a democracy.[2]

However, alarm bells are ringing increasingly loudly, but not to proclaim liberty. They do not move us to celebrate individual freedom as we once enjoyed; rather, they should jolt us to the kind of sacrificial action taken by Colonial minute-men when Paul Revere made his famous ride. Georgie Anne Geyer, in *Americans No More,* writes about the silent but real death of American citizenship. She relates the perceptive and prophetic speech at the Aspen Institute in Berlin in 1991 by the then Secretary of State James Baker III. He reminded the audience that the United States is "a nation of ideas, not of blood, birth, or creed, but a nation of self-affirming citizens consorting with one another and empowering their government to act for their benefit." Ms. Geyer proceeds to document disconcerting indicators that immigrants are increasingly not being assimilated into American citizenship. She further warns that America, "once unified, coherent and law-abiding, will become a crowded, bickering, highly criminalized incoherent nation." She believes that citizenship will be overtaken by group rights and that sense of responsibility for the community, or civic potency, will die.[3]

Newt Gingrich teaches that America is an idea (a belief shared by James Baker and stated elsewhere as a "proposition"). He says: "To be an American is to embrace a set of values and living habits that have flourished on this continent for nearly 400 years." In mid-1960, this consensus began to flounder. Multiculturalism resulted in a switch from proclaiming allegiance to the common culture to so-called virtues of particular ethnicity, sect, or tribe.[4]

Will our salvation depend on our public schools? We must not assume that the American public school system is a "dead letter," as has been concluded by the conservative Heritage Foundation and the left-liberal Brookings Institute. Rather than design an entirely new system of public education, as they recommend, we should focus on renewing the one we now have. Despite the endless criticism and past reform efforts, we must seek to remodel our school system rather than force parents to educate their children at home, resort to charter schools, or enroll in voucher programs.

E.D. Hirsch concluded that the ultimate success of school reform depends on the development of a skeptical, well-informed press, the general public, and the educational community, to oppose "dressed-up old ideas to look new."[5] This notion is in harmony with the theme of this book. Diane Ravitch also reminds us that whatever happens in the schools is determined by our assumptions, our ideals, and our policies, and they are what we choose to make them.[6] Thomas Sowell agrees that all the ingredients for a successful educational system already exists in the United States. Changing the institutions is the key.[7]

But it is a political task.

CHAPTER 3

Protecting Schools from
Dedicated Folly, Dogmas, and
Other Educational Nostrums

Throughout history men have sought to protect and maintain ownership and control of whatever they highly valued. This human attribute is evidenced today in bank vaults, property fences, and home and automobile security systems. Ironically, there is little evidence of concern about forces and influences that will inevitably destroy our public school system. If we believe that free public education is a "pearl of great price," no effort should be spared to insure its protection.

Americans hasten to criticize poor school conditions and educational outcomes, but are not equally outspoken about outrageous legislation, movements, trends and research studies that reach ridiculous conclusions relative to cause and effect—all of which mitigate against educational renewal.

Educational philosophy has shaped the structure of school systems and provides the basis for planning and decision-making. Education is a state function; each state school board maintains a written statement of beliefs to serve in the formulation of educational platforms relevant to each local system in the several states. All branches of state government should work in concert to serve as a buffer against any movement or influence that might jeopardize the effective operation of public education.

Our behaviors are shaped by trial and error, and by new discoveries of nature's laws, along with physical and psychological forces. Our experiences help teach what works and what does not, and we make progress when we discard what does not work. Educational planning, as in any human endeavor, should rely on historical knowledge, experience, sound scientific research, and administrative feasibility. In our time, we seem to have ignored these criteria and are suffering the agony of the consequences.

Could anyone have predicted the hair-brained schemes imposed on public schools since 1957? Thomas Sowell points to dogmas and numerous hidden agendas reflected in buzz-words that dominate educational policy—without evidence being either asked for or given to substantiate the beliefs they represent.[1] Such world-saving crusades have increasingly intruded into the classroom, crowding out basic skills. (Examples are noted below.) These impositions often originate in the Office of Education, by Acts of Congress, or are reflected in textbooks and instructional materials as a result of influence by special interest groups.

The panic that set in when Sputnik was launched produced a plethora of math, science, and foreign language programs in a frenzied effort to catch up with the Russian space program. Other than focus attention on shortcomings in these subject areas and effect the beginning of an era of major federal funding for education, curriculum programs formulated earlier have produced minimal benefits. We have subsequently suffered through similar panic attacks during the periods of integration, civil rights, racial quotas, feminism, political correctness, and the spawning of such well-intentioned, but ineffectual, experimentation in cross-town busing, outcome-based education, magnet schools, main-streaming, self-esteem education, multicultural-ism, American history revision, and misguided programs for disadvantaged students.

Among other beliefs that parents express about public schools are these two overriding expectations: that high academic standards are maintained, and that students will be taught in a physically safe environment. The danger they most fear is from abuse, assaults, and violence within the student population. The power of the school has been seriously circumscribed. There is, now, limited penalty or consequence for inappropriate behavior, few suspensions or expulsions, or removal of students who make learning next to impossibie for others.

Students do not normally choose to be incorrigible, delinquent, or antisocial. But such youth should not be considered educable within the structure that public schools can reasonably be expected to operate. We should continue to determine causes of such behavior and, at the earliest age, apply shaping measures to help these youngsters learn to function properly in our society. Unlike public school administrators, private and parochial school administrators do not normally spend inordinate time dealing with students that comprise only five percent of the total student population.

School administrators should provide parents written copies of approved school policies, regulations, and codes of conduct. When parents or guardians are required to sign a copy that is placed in their child's school file, they should be considered to be fully responsible for their child's behavior.

A practice of *zero tolerance* should be followed. Public schools should be protected from disruption by maintaining separate, alternative schools for unruly students.[2] These classes or schools should be staffed with teachers uniquely trained and qualified to meet the special needs of learning disabled students. A program of psychological testing, personal and group counseling, and parent or guardian involvement should be integral components of such programs.

The standard curriculum should be offered at an instructional pace to accommodate ability and achievement levels with provision for remedial activities as needed. Students may be reassigned to their regular schools when they demonstrate such behavior and attitude as to accommodate codes of conduct set in the regular school.

Citizens should exercise ownership rights to their schools and exert necessary power to ensure that schools will be allowed to focus full attention and energy on providing quality education.

CHAPTER 4

School Prayer and
The First Amendment

There is no more controversial or explosive issue than prayer in our public schools. In 1963, the Supreme Court ruled against school prayer, which, in varying degrees, was practiced in public schools since the Colonial period. Ironically, rather than "banning" recognition of America's religious heritage, the intention of the court was to encourage public schools to systematically and effectively teach about our religious heritage. What subsequently shaped judicial decisions and public school practices, however, was an onslaught of prohibitions against any semblance of religion.

Many contend that judicial rulings following the earlier Supreme Court ruling did not drive morality out of the schools. Gene Owens, political journalist for the *Mobile Register*, reflected this point of view in pointing out that when prayer was a part of school life there was evidence of immorality, particularly among students; but it was limited due to restraints set by families and oversight in closer-knit communities. He attributes moral decline to such villains as scattered neighborhoods, multi-car families, lack of parental supervision, rising affluence, two-parent bread-winners, perversion in the media, birth control, misguided welfare, and white flight.[1] However, we should allow that family influences that set limitations and community oversight in previous generations emerged from an educational system where Bibles were commonplace on teachers' desks, and in many states, Bible reading was required. If we accept the proposition that public schools are even partly responsible for perpetuating our culture and values, we must reasonably conclude that court rulings have created a moral vacuum in our schools.

Since 1963, on every societal front, nonsense is replacing good sense in our once-pragmatic nation. We have lived through a period that William J. Bennett expressed as substantial social regression. He cites in his Index of Leading Cultural Indicators that, since 1960, there has been a 560 percent increase in violent crime, 400 percent increase in illegitimate births, a quadrupling in divorce rates, a tripling of the percentage of children living in single-parent homes, and a 200 percent increase in teenage suicides.[2]

The examples of bad taste and behavior that we see are not isolated and unconnected. Martin Gross sees the social and cultural madness as part of a distinct national pattern. He attributes this movement to the New Establishment, a system of "social individualization," in which the rights of each person are more important than rights of the total group. This Establishment fills the spiritual void in millions who no longer believe in either Christianity or Judaism, yet insist on a faith larger than themselves and hold to a secular religion.[3] Angelo Codevilla refers to such a group as elitists. They seek to remake American culture in their own image. They accomplish their objectives in schools and in government, and are brilliantly marketed systematically through every possible outlet from newspapers to films, and from Broadway to television. Religious belief surveys, by occupation, show a concentration of "non-believers" among non-scientific academics, lawyers, civil servants, and those in the media, arts, and entertainment industries. When such elites refer to people who actually believe in the Nicene Creed or Jewish faith, they tend to use adjectives such as "ultra" or "fundamentalists" or describe them as being from the "religious right."[4]

The correlation between our moral decline and absence of moral instruction in schools is all too obvious, and it should not be assumed to be mere coincidence. The practice of offering prayer in schools has been a symbolic exercise in a shaping process to imbue children with Judeo-Christian beliefs and to help them internalize the principle of obedience to the sovereignty of the God acknowledged in our Declaration of Independence.

Referring to our cultural breakdown, Barbara Reynolds wrote in a recent column in *USA Today*,

> Those murderous habits aren't based on financial poverty, but on a bankrupt human spirit caused by an absence of the spirit of God. If it weren't for the religious faithful in cities and schools, life would be utterly hopeless....
>
> The downhill drag started in 1963 when the court kicked prayer out of the public schools. Our moral foundation crumbled, violent rap music, drugs, guns, and illicit sex leaped into the vacuum. While I don't want mandated prayers, you must find ways for schools and the workplace to implement values based on love, justice, and moral principles most religions adhere to.[5]

Americans are shocked at the increasing amount of violence on school campuses, and wanton slaughter of innocent students by troubled youth. Knee-jerk elitists, short on history and long on ability to promote their self-serving agendas, are given voice on major television stations. From this bully-pit, they propose a range of causes, from guns and lack of gun control, inadequate school security, violent video games and movies, lax discipline in schools, to the idea that children are "wired" at birth for evil. Deep down, most Americans know the root cause is that the locus of morality has shifted from the family to the state. They would have applauded to hear presidential candidate Alan Keyes, in a heated debate on a recent Fox News broadcast, exclaim, "I'd like to sue the judges that took God Almighty out of our public schools."

The Supreme Court has not done an admirable job in meeting its responsibility to maintain a proper balance between "Church and State." The resulting situation has been described as a tangled mess. The precarious position of public schools is due to less than scholarly adjudication. Some Supreme Court Justices have simply overlooked or ignored what our founding fathers intended the First Amendment to say. The slogan, "complete separation of Church and State," has been proclaimed so often and loudly that it seems to have become the sole basis of recent court rulings. Those who disagree have been bullied into believing its legality and that it should not be questioned. Completely overlooked is consideration for the second part of the First Amendment—namely, congressional action that would prohibit "free exercise of religion." That the expression "Church and State" is not found in our Constitution or Bill of Rights is also disregarded. When Jefferson used the phrase in a letter to a representative of Baptist and Congregational churches in Danbury, CT, he was expressing a belief to which he and other founding fathers held. They were well educated and knew the tragic consequences of a state-church government. Nevertheless, for the past 30 years our Supreme Court has relied on this principle to prohibit any Judeo-Christian influence, however non-denominational, in our public schools. This prompted one Supreme Court scholar, Chief Justice William Rehnquist, to remark, "The wall of separation between church and state is a metaphor based on bad history, a metaphor which has proved useless as a guide to judging. It should be frankly and implicitly abandoned."[6]

Lino Graglia believes that the rule of law and practice and the Supreme Court rulings have nothing to do with the text of the Constitution or the intention of those who wrote it, but rather reflect the political preferences of judges and their associates off the bench.[7] Sadly, the tangled mess of clouded judicial legislation is reflected in such conflicting practices as use of tax funds to buy textbooks for nonpublic schools, for bus transportation, and release time for public school teachers for specialized instruction. It is argued that such tax monies are legal and justified because they go to directly benefit students rather than the non-public schools.

In 1995, a collaborative statement was signed by the American Civil Liberties Union (ACLU) and 30 religious and civic organizations outlining religious rights of students in public schools. This document states that:

- Students may pray individually or in informal groups if no disruption is caused; teachers and school administrators cannot encourage religious activity;
- Students may be taught about religion, the role of religion in United States history, but not given religious instruction;
- Students may discuss religion with their peers but not harass them;
- Schools can celebrate only the secular aspects of religious holidays; and
- They can be taught civic virtues but not their religious bases.

One might be persuaded that the issue is not merely the act of praying in school, but is part of an invidious crusade to eliminate any aspect of religious belief from our schools, and eventually, America. The so-called "religious rights" in the aforementioned statement diverts attention away from an increasing number of federal and state judicial rulings that prohibit non-denominational religious activities in public schools, such as:

- Saying grace in class before lunch
- Displaying the Ten Commandments
- Offering non-denominational prayer at school events
- Wearing the Star of David, a cross, or other religious symbols and slogans
- Presenting book reports and research papers on religious topics

One cannot rule out the close correlation between the Supreme Court's decision and the subsequent decline of the over-all moral climate in America. Many acknowledge that we are in a culture war. If so, we must conclude that the foundation of so-called "family values"—perpetuated heretofore by our public schools—is being eroded. The actions of groups that could cause societal decay seem to be based on a misguided, biased interpretation of separation of church and state and freedom of speech, which is the theme of this chapter.

School children are taught that Columbus sailed west from Spain in 1492 to search for material riches, as did other adventurers from European countries. Settlements by these nations left social customs and practices unique to their countries, but none influenced the development of ideals of individual freedom, freedom of religion, and representative democracy which later emerged. The seeds of such ideals were sown by the first colonists who emigrated from England, Holland, and Scotland. They were educated and understood the political principles and practices of centuries of Anglo-Saxon rule. They brought to these shores the rich cultural and educational heritage of Western Europe, along with their fervent hope for religious freedom. Historians generally mark the beginning of American history with these permanent settlements and, with them, the formulation of values and beliefs reflected in our Constitution and

Bill of Rights, subsequently shaping the unique culture that we define as American.

In contrast to the way other nations developed in the history of the world, America was founded on a proposition, summed up in the four documents: the Declaration of Independence, the Constitution of the United States, the Bill of Rights, and the Northwest Ordinance. Our federal and state governments were founded upon principles—held by the founders, from their knowledge of the Scriptures—beliefs reflected in that proposition—and from which religion cannot be separated.

Prior to the Constitutional Convention in 1787, a small group of patriots, including George Washington, Benjamin Franklin, Edmond Randolph, James Madison, and Robert Morris, agreed to write a constitution for a government based on the consent of the governed, and the rights of the people would flow from God. Our Constitution is remarkable, shaped within a context of Judeo-Christian influence. Because of the various religious denominations that existed even then, it was not felt practical or desirable to establish a national school system on religious bases. But those who voted to ratify our Constitution did not intend to separate religion from education. This belief was clearly embedded in the Northwest Ordinance, adopted in 1787, which emphasized the need for religion and morality along with education.

In 1833, in his Commentaries on the Constitution, Justice Story, in referring to the First Amendment, maintained that its purpose was "to prevent any national ecclesiastical establishment that should give to a hierarchy the exclusive patronage of the national government." He explained that the First Amendment was not intended to be unfriendly to religion, but to preserve an equity between sects, and, most importantly, to leave religion up to the states.[8] Although the "wall of separation" metaphor may be a useless guide to judging, for the past 30 years our Supreme Court has continually relied on it to prohibit any Judeo-Christian influence, however non-denominational, in our public schools.

Our belief that we live in the freest country in the world is well founded, but we are more and more deprived of the freedom to choose between moral schools and secular humanist schools. During the past three decades there has been an acknowledged close relationship between a public school system devoid of moral education, and moral decline in our society. What has been described as a "cultural war" has been raging during this period. One might easily conclude that efforts are being made not merely to make schools secular by removing value education from the curriculum, but to actually replace value education with secular humanism.

The Freedom of Religion aspect of the First Amendment has been under attack since the Civil War. American citizens do not want our government or public schools to promote a particular religious denomination, but they do want moral education, shaped from religious belief, as an integral part of school life. Such was considered by our Supreme Court in the landmark *McCollum Religious Case* in 1947. It dealt with an association of Jewish, Roman Catholic and Protestant faiths to conduct voluntary classes in religious education in public school buildings during class time. It was ruled unconstitutional. J.M. O'Neill, in his *Religion and Education Under the Constitution*, noted that "the Supreme Court gave up the first clause of the First Amendment without firing a shot in defense of the work of Jefferson and Madison, and as defended earlier by the Supreme Court." What this school district tried to do was to offer a reasoned and practical approach that could contribute to ending the war over religion in the public schools. They worked to incorporate a strand of instruction based on doctrine common to Catholic, Protestant, and Jewish faiths, cooperatively developed by clergy, priests, and a Rabbi from the local community.[9]

The teaching of religion in Great Britain's public schools was accomplished through a similar program; namely, the development of the *Agreed Syllabus*, with the full concurrence and support of the three major faiths. This approach might yet serve as a model for replication in school systems throughout our country.

Fortunately, the demand by responsible citizens to "take back our country" is growing more intense, but we must first retrieve our schools. Religion, as proclaimed by like-minded atheistic groups in keeping with their political agendas, is not the responsibility of our schools. Acknowledging that moral development is first the responsibility of parents, the majority of Americans believe that "family values" should be reflected in the "warp and woof" of life in our public schools. Conceptualization about religion is basic to a liberal education—the kind of education that should prepare students to function as good citizens in American democracy. We delude ourselves if we hope to separate religion from mathematics, science, literature, art, music, health, history, economics, government, or any other educational discipline. Education has to do with acquiring knowledge, but it is more about the application of knowledge reflected in behavior.

This issue will be resolved when there is collegial action between Congress and the Supreme Court—based on a revised interpretation of the First Amendment through the eyes of the men who wrote it. This action should reestablish a legal basis for adjudication to allow prayer and religion their proper place in our schools.

PART THREE

Teachers:
Good, Marginal,
and Incompetent

CHAPTER 5

Teacher Preparation

More and more money is not the answer to solving the problems of public education. Admittedly, there must be adequate funding to administer the range of administrative functions. And money obviously plays a part—this is observed when good teachers and school administrators gravitate to school districts that offer higher salaries, more resources, and better working conditions. Educational reformers believe that more money needs to be spent. Analysis of American high schools by John Chubb and Terry Moe confirm that financial resources do not matter much, except in cases of extreme deprivation or gross abundance.[1] Thomas Sowell's research also points to the lack of correlation between "financial inputs and weak and shaky educational outputs." He believes that the reason spending has so little effect on educational performance is that most of the money never reaches the classroom.[2] The argument tendered here, however, is that resources are not channeled to ensure quality teacher-training programs.

By all indicators—whether objective data or first-hand observation—the intellectual caliber of public school teachers in the United States is shockingly low. For decades, college students who have majored in education have been among the least qualified of all college students.

Chester Finn points to one enduring bit of folk wisdom about American education. It must be understood that courses given by teacher-education programs are near worthless in their own right and consume so much time that there is little time left to learn subjects they will be one day teaching.[3]

Not too encouraging is Hirsch's reminder that, although some teachers are educated in research universities, most are trained in non-research institutions. Critics and defenders of schools of education agree that, as a group, professors of education are held in low esteem by their colleagues. What has dominated the process of teacher education he refers to as the "American Thoughtworld"—a juggernaut that crushes independence of mind. His critical description of a series of harmful teacher training philosophies include: lack of academic vigor; progressive education; negative attitudes about teaching factual information; that we cannot be compared to better schools in other countries; unwarranted attention to student uniqueness and anti-intellectualism.[4]

"Good teaching makes for good learning" is an axiom accepted throughout the recorded history of education. Students learn when teachers know the subject matter, use sound teaching methodology, and teach with urgency and enthusiasm. Except for a few notable efforts to address the cause of our educational problems, we have avoided the issue of teacher training. Arguably, this is the result of ignorance on the part of the lay community and the considerable influence of the National Education Association and local teachers' unions.

Hirsch refers us to a significant but seldom-discussed study by James Popham. In his *Performance Tests of Teaching Proficiency*, he exposed the lack of nuts-and-bolts pedagogical training in education schools. He pointed to the failure to instruct prospective teachers about the best research into effective pedagogical methods. Education schools do not convey to teachers the research that shows the superior effectiveness of clear focus, definite standards, diligent practice, and continual monitoring through tests and other evaluation measures.[5]

The era following "Sputnik" spawned a plethora of federally funded programs purported to help the embarrassed public school system catch up with the Russians; but their focus was implementation of specific courses rather than improvement of teaching quality. The range of compensatory programs, later put in place to remediate the ills of segregation, has proven more beneficial to politicians than students.

Thus, as stated heretofore, we have avoided dealing with the real issue. Such proposed changes include:

- Lengthening the school year,
- Requiring higher achievement standards,
- Increasing the number of units for graduation,
- Implementing magnet schools,
- Offering parents choice of schools with voucher plans,
- Installing computers in all classrooms, and
- Designing unrealistic teacher evaluation programs that attack the symptoms rather than the root cause.

Accountability in public education and educational reform will not be achieved until we come to grips with the root cause.

We should demand that state governors, state boards of education and other appropriate elected officials enact or revise legislation to strengthen the total process of teacher training, testing, certification, evaluation, promotion, and termination.

What a teacher is, according to typical state laws relating to education, is one who has been certified by the state teacher certification office. Such status is achieved by submitting documentation of the baccalaureate degree and satisfactory completion of a specific body of educational courses from an approved teacher-training college or university. But teacher training varies *markedly* among these institutions in curriculum content, course standards, quality of the faculty, and the general nurture of intellectual development.

Jobs in most work places carry job descriptions, written or implied, for the work to be done. Except for a broad range of general expectancies, specific job descriptions are not attached to such professions as physicians, lawyers, clergy, and teachers. However, it is usual for specific practices and procedures, accepted by the profession for specific functions, to be strictly followed. Ironically, this is not true for the teaching profession.

The "education establishment" is faulted for fiercely defending the need for pedagogical training while rebuking studies that show such training makes no difference. Twenty states have reported that some form of alternative certification has been enacted to allow military retirees and others with limited teacher training to teach.[6] Because the body of teaching pedagogy is alleged to make no difference, it has not been given a chance, and therefore does not deserve its questionable reputation. In fact, instruction is ineffective because most teachers have not been properly instructed in sound teaching practices and pedagogy based on scientific research; teacher training is simply not reflected in most classrooms.

Few educators have contributed more to help America's teachers teach better and faster than Dr. Madeline Hunter. She maintains that teaching pedagogy remains unused because it is written in language more familiar to statisticians and lies buried in research journals in university libraries. Such knowledge, when appropriately applied, can highly predict teaching success.[7]

Curricula in most teacher-training schools include such courses as *Human Growth and Development, Educational Psychology*, and *Teaching Methods*—the body of knowledge critical to the status of teaching as a true profession. However, the background gained from such courses is not generally reflected in day-to-day teaching practices. Courses that could be better taught in academic departments are offered in teacher training programs as special courses for elementary or secondary teachers. It is no wonder that what is called "education courses" has earned disdain by the general public.

Ironically the body of disciplines—behavioral psychology, human growth and development, and learning principles—does not constitute a significant amount of time in most teacher preparation programs. Such knowledge has evolved over thousands of years and characterizes teaching as a profession. They should be understood, internalized, practiced, and demonstrated under competent supervision before a teacher trainee is approved for "student teaching" and recommended for certification. To require that a few principles of learning only be memorized rather than become a basic set of teaching tools is analogous to teaching aviators to fly only in ground school.

CHAPTER 6

Teacher Certification

W hat does it mean to be a certified teacher? Maybe not much? Teaching has been referred to as the noblest of professions. Those who devote their lives to teaching are proud of what they do. More people belong to the teaching profession than any other occupation, and we rely on them to pass on to each succeeding generation knowledge, skills, and attitudes to help them live successfully in an increasingly complex society.

The general decline of public education and educational performance cannot be attributed solely to teachers. We must critically examine the full complement of entities responsible for teacher quality. The certification badge that teachers wear is their primary passport through the door to the classroom.

"I don't have to study because there are no examinations." "We are graded on class participation." Robert Bork reported that this practice was revealed to him by an education student during exam week in 1953.[1] This example of the lack of rigor and scholarship reflected in teacher-training institutions, we hope, is an extreme one. For if not, this condition will inevitably be reflected in teacher certification standards.

Physicians, attorneys, and other professional personnel undergo comprehensive certification examinations before being allowed to practice in each state. To protect the general welfare, most trade vocations require that rigid state and municipal certification standards be met. Teachers, in contrast, may receive approval to teach based only on credentials and transcripts approved by the college or university where the training was received. State departments of education approve colleges to offer teacher training based primarily on teacher training programs they offer, along with credentials of their instructional staffs. Oversight by the State is maintained by sporadic inspections at the universities, with limited classroom observation, and little guarantee that the school's graduates will perform at the level expected by state departments of education or school districts that employ the teachers.

In 1963, James Conant, in his landmark *A Nation at Risk*, called for drastic changes in teacher education that would make the university solely responsible for teacher preparation, free from state certification requirements. This was his most controversial recommendation and, fortunately, it was not well received. His other suggestions, such as more flexible preparation programs, greater emphasis on general education, better student teaching programs, and controlled periods of probationary service, harmonize with more acceptable reform measures.

As in many reform movements, however, there are efforts to supplant existing practices, rather than actually reform or bring about renewal. This is seen in the movement described by Chester Finn that allows for "alternative teacher certification." He sees this approach as a way to attract and keep more able and better qualified people in teaching. Mid-career and college graduates with degrees in academic fields would be provided with on-the-job supervision, mentoring and pointers on classroom craftsmanship. Only those who do well would be retained.[2] (We wish that this were possible in dealing with certified marginal teachers.)

Another program that would supplement, and might possibly replace, state certification programs is one endorsed by the National Board for Professional Teaching that would provide for national certification. The goal of this effort is to restructure public school teaching around a new set of professional standards of knowledge that can be codified and transmitted to new practitioners. Some aspects of the program:

- Certification would be immune from state-level political squabbling.
- It would be optional.
- It would be available to experienced teachers who want additional credential testimony to their professional expertise.
- Certification would be awarded to teachers who have demonstrated their knowledge through written examination, videotapes, classroom observation and interviews.[3]

It can be argued that such proposals, in addition to creating additional levels of bureaucracy, offer no more promising solutions to improve the certification problem than can be achieved by strengthening measures that are currently in place. (Such measures are suggested in Chapter 29.)

We should not blame teachers for the certification problem. It is true that teacher competency tests have shown embarrassing results in most school districts where they have been given.

Diane Ravitch believes that the rush to attack teachers for the ills of public education smacks of more than a little scapegoating. Why not blame colleges and universities for lowering entrance requirements or businesses and employers for setting up multi-million-dollar programs to train basic skills? Instead, she states, the blame should be shared by the public, school boards, legislatures, the press, and the federal government,

which collectively narrowed the teachers' professional autonomy in the classroom. Her finger of blame is also pointed at
courts for whittling away at the schools' ability to maintain
safety and order, education departments for requiring vapid
education courses, and local school boards for a mountain of
bureaucratic regulations.[4]

Certification problems probably will not be resolved in
isolation from remedies applied to teacher training and teacher
evaluation. But we should not seek to abandon the framework
now in place and replace it with fanciful and unproven practices
that may be worse.

CHAPTER 7

Teacher Evaluation

We recall Socrates' admonition: "The unexamined life is not worth living." This is true of our lives and is applicable in every aspect of our existence. Both private and public institutions are continually evaluated in the marketplace and rewarded or penalized accordingly by the consumers to whom they provide products or services. Ironically, this principle is not stringently applied to teachers and administrators in our public schools. Moreover, the evaluative measures applied to educators are not always suitable to make good schools more probable. Although not totally responsible, teacher unions hamper progress when they oppose the practice of evaluating teachers, and work to "water-down" procedures that might be put in place to measure good teaching. Judicial rulings have also deterred implementation of needed evaluation procedures.

Presently, there is hue and cry for teacher ratings based on student test scores. Such data, however important, should only serve to *support* subjective observations distilled from a reliable teacher observation process. That is the essence of this chapter.

Some generalizations about teacher competence may be made when students are grouped homogeneously in similar physical settings and when teacher assignments remain the same. But even in such settings, there are too many influences that could affect the reliability of any measure. Also, the neurological and complex variability of human beings will always prevent the use of such a subjective evaluation instrument based solely on student learning.[1]

Some of the myths that serve as obstacles to teaching evaluation include: All teachers are alike and should be treated the same; the teaching act is too obscure, complex, and it is impossible to evaluate the components of quality teaching. Also, it is believed that the highest salaries should go to those with the most academic credits or most years in service.[2]

Teaching is both a science and an art. The teaching act is not easily evaluated by an *untrained* observer. Descriptions of good teaching have always included such attributes as personality, attitude, value orientation, and motivation. Such qualities, however, are highly subjective.

What is needed is a set of scientifically based criteria to assess the aspect of teaching that we insist is scientific—behaviors that are embodied in principles that make up the body of teaching pedagogy.

There are countless additional factors that mitigate efforts to make schools better, but there seems to be absence of widespread thought that the root cause may be in the rank and file of marginal and incompetent teachers.

The belief supported here is that teacher evaluation should be based primarily on what teachers *do*—specific teaching acts in specific situations. This is not a new point of view. It has been advanced by nationally recognized educators based on extensive teaching research data collected and disseminated by Dr. Madeline Hunter and her associates at the University of California at Los Angeles. The typical teacher evaluation instrument and evaluation process frequently used includes an extensive checklist of criteria *extraneous to factors essential to effective teaching*. She has reduced the myriad of such checklist items to those that consider only factors essential to effective teaching—entirely pedagogical. Rather than recommend a standard teacher evaluation instrument, the purpose here is to strongly advise that any form intended to reliably assess effective teaching should include a small section of criteria that will yield the following information:

- Does the teacher demonstrate sound knowledge of the subject matter?
- Is the teacher teaching to a specific learning objective?
- Is the objective appropriate for the particular learning session?
- Are appropriate learning principles being correcly applied?
- Are materials and equipment in use appropriate to meet stated learning objectives?
- Are students continually monitored to adjust the pace of instruction, and level of difficulty, to ensure that learning is taking place?
- Are appropriate evaluation procedures used?

This body of observation criteria is applicable in all teaching situations—all grade levels, all subject areas, small or large classes, homogeneous or heterogeneous, and for students of all atypical designations.

The focus on what the teacher does in applying sound teaching pedagogy is analogous to approved medical procedures that surgeons are required to follow in specific operations. When painters mix blue and yellow colors they believe that some shade of green will result—every time. When medicine is approved for use by our Food and Drug Administration (FDA), enough research has been done to assure that beneficial results of its use are highly probable.

When instructional methodology
is correctly applied, we should be able to
make the same kind of predictions.

Observations of teachers at work in classrooms is a quality control measure. Teachers should not consider this practice as restrictive, inhibiting, a demonstration of lack of trust, or unprofessional. Rather, when teachers are aware of standards that must be met, that the supervisor is as competent as they are, they can become partners in the process of continuous school improvement. Artistry in the supervisory process is seen when agreement is mutually reached regarding steps the teacher will take to improve.

PART FOUR

Struggle for Survival

CHAPTER 8

School Vouchers

School vouchers are a "last gasp" reform movement that would allow use of federal or state tax monies for students to attend private, parochial, or public schools outside their assigned attendance area. The case for school vouchers as an educational choice is compelling. It is gaining widespread acceptance along with efforts to enact legislation to legalize such a practice. It is not, however, new. In 1955, Milton Friedman had recommended that parents should be given chits, or vouchers, to cash in as tuition at any school to which they chose to send their children.[1] One prominent federal legislator stated that school choice is going to shake up the current political order at its very foundation as parents seek relief from failing and dangerous schools. This movement will be propelled increasingly forward as a result of the United States Supreme Court's recent decision not to review a challenge to a Wisconsin law that provides tuition vouchers for private education, including parochial schools.

As underscored elsewhere, parents do not necessarily believe the voucher system will cure educational problems. But because they feel powerless to effect change, they welcome the option it provides. Out of desperation, parents will try any reform plan that seems enticing because they are not aware of the cause of the problem or just how to fix it.[1] Reforms tried in the past two generations, with few exceptions, have not resulted in improving public schools.[2] More money has not made a measurable difference. Private and parochial schools continue to out-perform public schools on standardized achievement tests. Ninety-eight percent of Americans support some kind of school choice. Fifty-six percent support vouchers to any school of their choice. Forty-two percent support vouchers only within public schools. Dr. Chester Finn, one of America's most respected public school spokesmen, reluctantly stated that, while private schools were more effective and economical than public schools, focus should be placed on the winnable campaign for choice within public schools.[3] The growing acceptance of, and efforts to legalize, voucher plans is based on a belief that such plans will bring about:

- Improved education for students trapped in marginal inner-city schools,
- Redeemable "chits" or tax credits based on family income and
- Credit to attend parochial schools, which is not judged to violate the Church and State Amendment because grants go to parents rather than parochial schools.

Many consider the major advantage of private schools to be freedom from state and federal guidelines or requirements relating to teaching and learning, and meaningless, time-consuming reports.

But compelling arguments can be made against school voucher plans:

- Competition between schools from which students transfer will not result in improvement without the implementation of renewal measures. Schools that are poorly administered and staffed with marginal teachers serving students from dysfunctional families and economically deprived communities will not have the resources or power to compete.

- Loss of funds to public schools will require additional taxes or reduction of personnel, school maintenance, transportation, and other essential services.
- Parents of students who could benefit from better education may not choose to transfer them to a voucher school.
- A separate bureaucracy may emerge to administer details of a voucher system that may prove to be more complex and expensive than anticipated.
- Better administrators and teachers will migrate to better voucher schools
- The voucher school may not accommodate learning disabled students or those with physical or emotional handicaps.
- Teacher unions will lobby against voucher legislation.
- Use of tax monies will result in federal oversight and management of private and parochial schools that currently enjoy freedom from control by the U.S. Department of Education.

Charles Willie, of Harvard University, argues that for the choice plan to succeed everyone must be forced to make a choice; otherwise educational interests are held hostage by real estate interests. Therefore, the neighborhood school would have to be eliminated. He maintains that "unless *everyone* chooses, you have a system of *choosers* and *non-choosers*, and you cannot control for self-selection."[4]

Our high regard for private and parochial schools is not misplaced. They provide a valuable alternative to public schools for parents who want more control of educational outcomes or specific religious training. Such schools boast high student achievement, minimum student disruption and a more tightly controlled learning environment, which they achieve at less cost. A stern warning, however, was issued by Anne Stewart Connell, columnist for *The Wanderer*, the Catholic weekly publication. She cautioned private schools against bargaining away their souls for government money. "What will happen," she said, "to Catholic children when parochial schools may be inundated by a majority of children who share no similar religious values?" Spokesperson for conservative issues Phyillis Schlafly has also criticized the movement to centralize schools under federal control and transform private schools into public institutions.

To a great extent, we have already abandoned public education by virtue of our neglecting to protect it from 30 years of debilitating influences and movements. To divert tax funds for vouchers would be analogous to using tax funds to support private militia groups if our regular armed forces were deemed not competent to defend our country.

John Chubb and Terry Moe agree that school choice in its proposed form is not a panacea. It does not change the fundamental way in which the system has operated—*under traditional governance*. They believe that, while school choice offers a break from the institutional past, it comes from the same mold as other reforms—granting parents additional options or giving schools more incentives to compete *without changing the system in any fundamental way*;

> Our guiding principle in the design of a choice system is this: Public authority must be put to use in creating a system that is almost entirely beyond the reach of public authority. Because states have primary responsibility for American public education, we think the best way to achieve significant, enduring reform is for states to take the initiative in withdrawing

authority from existing institutions and building a new system in which most authority is vested directly in the schools, parents, and students.[5]

Their version of choice is a self-contained reform with its own rationale and justification. (This is in harmony with the theme of this book. However, while they base their panacea on theory, recommendations herein are believed to be based on principles and experience.) Their proposal would redefine what a "public school" is, and create what we have come to know as charter schools. The state would set criteria for schools that qualify, and those schools would be granted authority to determine their own governing structure.[6]

It is hoped that we will choose the option to shore-up the framework of the structure of public education we now have.

Our schools did not fall into disrepair entirely because of failure from within. It is the source of influences from without the school establishment that contributed to its present condition, and these are the sources on which we will probably depend to bring about genuine reform.

Whereas many are attracted to the remedy of "school choice," the approach recommended here is to choose to improve our public schools rather than abandon them.

CHAPTER 9

Charter Schools

The charter school movement originated in Minnesota in 1991 as an alternative to public schools with the objective of making public schools more competitive. Approximately 800 such schools are currently in operation in twenty states. Approval to operate is based on charters they receive from their state education departments or from their local boards of education.

In contrast to private schools, charter schools enjoy autonomy with little oversight. Free from bureaucratic restraints, they are able to develop their own curriculum, select textbooks, and determine class size. Their attendance area is not circumscribed. Their teachers are not required to meet state certification standards. They do, however, receive state funds on a per-pupil basis, participate in the free and reduced price school lunch program and abide by health, safety, and non-discrimination regulations. They cannot offer any religious instruction.

Start-up schools may be established by parent groups who may be unhappy with public schools and want more local control of their children's education. They may lease space in public school buildings or other facilities that meet educational facility requirements.

Amy Stuart Wells predicted that choice schools, like charter schools, would predominate in the 1990s. In contrast to earlier choice schools, like magnet and voucher schools that focused on desegregation and better instruction, statewide charter schools are designed to infuse the free-market principles of competition into public education.[1] Some maintain, however, that the implicit analogy with economic competition is imperfect. There is sufficient evidence to show that parent choice has not greatly improved student achievement in the United States—that choice by itself is not an adequate principle reform; however, parents will send their children long distances to attend choice schools that offer truly good instruction.[2]

The success of charter schools is yet to be assessed. Such schools operate only where enabling legislation has been enacted, and the movement has not been observed to be growing rapidly. State legislation has been passed in California, Colorado, Georgia, Massachusetts, and New Mexico. By 1992, legislation to authorize charter schools was introduced in Alaska, Arizona, Connecticut, Florida, Michigan, New Jersey, Oregon, Pennsylvania, Tennessee, Vermont, and Wisconsin.[3]

Insurance costs and security bonding, along with legal aid requirements, add to the cost to operate charter schools. Because they compete with public schools for tax monies that would normally be allocated to public schools, local school boards, not to mention teacher unions, do not support them.

The charter school movement, though well-intended, has not received glowing reports. Scores on standardized achievement tests have not been significantly higher in charter schools than public schools and there have been no notable financial savings. Moreover, *lack of accountability* measures have resulted in cases of gross mismanagement and dishonesty, resulting in charter revocation.

In *U.S. News & World Report*, Thomas Toch wrote of his visits to nearly three dozen charter schools, which yielded a picture of *educational entrepreneurialism* featuring not only the classic benefits of any market-based enterprise, but the classic drawbacks as well. They are both better *and worse* than public schools, beset with problems as severe as—and in some cases, worse than—those found in public schools.[4]

As is true for the school voucher movement, charter schools do not offer a viable solution to failing public schools unless appropriate renewal measures are put in place—the kind of measures that should be applied to public schools.

PART FIVE

Debilitating Influences

CHAPTER 10

Measuring Student Progress, Standardized Testing, and a National Testing Program

S tudent progress—how much is learned—must be continually measured. Good teachers continually evaluate student progress in a variety of formative and summative ways, including: oral questioning, class discussion with complete sentence responses, seat-work, homework, written reports, observation, quizzes, unit tests, and semester and year-end tests. Formative evaluation, rather than for reporting progress or for promotion purposes, should primarily serve to adjust instructional activities and level of instruction. Summative assessment should be used to report to parents, assign final grades, and provide information for promotion and retention.

Ongoing assessment should be an integral part of daily instruction, but such evaluation is unfortunately often limited to written "fill-in-the-blank," "matching," and sentence-completion answers to questions in the student's textbook, or teacher's manual. Thus, limited attention is given to tailoring and adjusting the learning setting to the unique needs of the student group, or to the wide range of learning experiences that children should have. Such information ought to provide data to adjust the teaching process, with attention to such concerns as pacing, review, drill, the need to re-teach, and level of difficulty. Care should be taken to "flag" curriculum content that may not be included in the basal textbook, but is required in the state and district courses of study.

Standardized Tests

Standardized tests are designed to measure learning outcomes in specific subject areas for groups of students, in contrast to tests used to assess individual student progress. Since World War II, the use of standardized tests has surged in response to demand for accountability and to measure the success of the explosive number of reform measures. Standardized tests have served us well when they were used properly, but furious attacks are currently being waged against their use from within and without the educational community.[1]

Standardized tests are administered in public schools nationwide. They serve to provide a common denominator of data about education in America. Some districts administer tests annually at all grade levels, but, this may be unnecessary in view of the "sampling" purpose of such tests. When used as a single indicator, they serve as a valid, consistent measure of comparing learning and educational achievement at the state and local levels, and with other developed countries throughout the world. Such tests are normed or averaged with large groups of students, and should not be used to compare or measure progress of individual students.

Often-noted complaints about standardized testing include: concern that teachers stress only test questions and neglect other important learning objectives; lack of test security; and inappropriate use and faulty interpretation of test results. Such shortcomings should not deter reaping rewards of standardized testing programs. Standardized test data can be used to answer such important questions as:

- Is all material tested reflected in the school curriculum?
- Is sufficient time allocated to teaching material included on the test, and is it taught prior to the time students are tested?
- What curriculum revision should be made?
- What materials, equipment, and special instructional materials are indicated?
- What teacher training activities are needed?

It is always necessary to understand that the typical standardized test is intended to sample only selected curriculum areas such as reading, math, and language.

Thoughtful educators maintain that assessment of student learning must include questions to elicit high order thinking skills that apply to academic, everyday, and novel situations, and should include a variety of test items that require sustained reasoning.[2]

While some criticisms of standardized tests are valid, we should not "shoot the messenger" or "throw out the baby with the bath water." Data from these tests are our greatest source of information about academic performance. Rather than using test information to aid in assessing efforts to remedy our educational ills, the education profession chooses to wage war on testing and the outcomes emphasis associated with it. Why? Because revealing the grave situation public education is in reflects badly on educators. It is argued that repeated criticisms of objective tests are simply not valid.[3] Abuses in test administration can easily be avoided by watchful educators and an informed public.

Minimum Competency Testing

Graduation rates are up. More students are taking more academic subjects, but the vast majority of American students are still educated at too low a level. Exit examinations, or minimum competency testing as a requirement for high school graduation, is the current high-profile reform movement to set higher standards. Gene Maeroff cites Denver, CO, as the birthplace of minimum competency testing in 1959. Irate businessmen had complained about high school graduates who were not mentally equipped to be productive workers. The movement picked up slowly during the 1960s and gained momentum during the 1970s as concern grew about the declining achievement that was sweeping the country. By the early 1980s, 36 states had adopted some sort of minimum competency testing.

Before 1950, prior to the era of "dumbed down" education, the high school diploma was hard-earned and considered to be a valid document. Minimum testing programs are expected to raise the diploma to its original currency. Exit testing emerged to assure the diploma meant graduates could read, write and compute at a specified level of competence—heretofore referred to as "survival skills." Tests are generally developed and administered by state departments of education, but in some areas this responsibility has been delegated to local school districts.

It may not be too early to predict that so-called "exit testing" will prove to be another idiotic, and political "band-aid" attempt to fix education. Substituting quantity of knowledge attained for quality of teaching and learning—teaching and learning more, not better—is the downfall of this approach. The level of minimum competencies varies from state to state and continues to be revised. Some standards are so low that they are meaningless or so high that they are unenforceable. More importantly, there is no reason to expect that students will achieve any set standard without changing the educational setting on which we rely to prepare them to be tested.

It is argued here that use of exit tests will probably do little to raise educational standards or improve student performance—particularly among those students whom this method is intended to help. The majority of students presently see exit tests as "a piece of cake."[4] For others, the alternative is to leave school without a diploma. As a consequence, practice in test-taking and supplemental tutoring programs are being activated to help students develop competencies they should have achieved in the regular school program.

John Chubb and Terry Moe share this opinion. Among other criticism, they believe that testing requirements are a lot like raising certification requirements and other traditional reforms. They seem to make good sense and offer some benefits but are clearly deficient as solutions to problems they address, and stand little chance of improving schools in any significant way.[5]

We depend on educational objectives and testing to drive the teaching process, but exit tests should not replace the "dip-sticking" function of standardized tests or formative assessment that may be gained from minimum competency testing.

In keeping with the prominent theme of this book, *the solution to our failing schools is to be found in* **the teaching act**, *not the testing act*. Our focus should be on what is taught and how it is taught—on sound teaching pedagogy and empowerment of teachers—not in testing.

A National Testing Program

The White House is currently advocating national testing in reading and math for fourth- and eighth-grade students. The variance in the level of achievement standards in America's 15,000 local schools is acknowledgement of the need for a national standard, but only as a level of achievement for states to reach on their own initiative. It can also be argued that a standard set by the federal government will not result in a higher level of student achievement. This, however, has not deterred our federal government from pursuing its effort to accomplish this objective, even in the face of resistance expressed at a recent governors' summit meeting. Conservatives submit that it threatens local control over what students should learn; liberals fear that the data will be used to further brand inner city students as inferior; and ethnic groups complain that the tests may not be given in languages other than English.

Eighty-eight percent of Americans favor a national testing program and the establishment of a national core curriculum as measures of accountability. National assessment is not a new idea. When the United States Office of Education was established in 1867, it was charged with, among other things, determining the progress of education in America. This office has always collected test data from the several states, but has never, itself, carried out a national testing program. The battle for this terrain has been fought ever since, with skirmishes over subject matter, assessment procedures, and how the test data will be reported and used.

In recent years, the move to institute a national test program has steadily gained momentum, due in part to the failure of organizations such as the federally funded National Association of Educational Progress to provide test data suitable to show how students were actually doing. With the endorsement of power groups such as the Chief State School Officers, and the National Governors' Association, along with the support of Presidents Reagan, Bush, Carter, and Clinton, a national testing program may soon prevail over forces marshalled against it.

President Clinton and his Education Secretary, Richard Riley, are moving headlong in the direction of creating national standards, national testing, and a national curriculum.[6] Our greatest challenge in restructuring public education is to achieve the benefits of national standards and standardized measurement tools while preserving and increasing community and parental choice, participation, and control and, even more important, avoiding greater government, particularly federal government, intervention. We must find a way to balance the cost and benefits of *centralization vs. decentralization.*

Glaring inconsistencies are noted in the current restructuring movement—we may well be headed for another era of "fragmented" centralization.

How will the national test results be used? More testing does not equal more, much less better, learning. With history as the guide, we should expect subsequent guidelines, mandatory regulations, and more waste of public tax monies. Not only will there be no increase in student achievement, but national testing may conflict with, or duplicate, testing programs now carried on in local school systems.

We can measure up to international competition without national educational standards or control by the federal government if appropriate reforms are put in place. Meaningful standards for each grade level and high school graduation requirements consistent throughout the nation should be controlled by each state. Standards evolve over time—they are our observations and measurements of past performance. They are continuously reflected in, and determined by, the content, scope and sequence of basal textbooks and teachers' lesson plans, and are measured by standardized tests currently in use. Such controls should remain the prerogative of state boards of education.

Overlooked by advocates of national standards and testing are the numerous national and regional agencies and associations that regularly meet to report, share research and information, and discuss ways to improve education in their respective regions. Such national and regional meetings make up a collegial network of representatives from such groups as state governors, state boards of education, state and local school superintendents, administrative and supervisory personnel, and subject area groups that include classroom teachers. These relationships are vital to a continuing process of homogenizing American education without federal intervention.

We depend on educational objectives to drive the educational process. Standards change and are needed to serve only as goals. The goals that our schools ultimately reach will depend on the quality of teachers and administrators, and this can only be achieved through legislative and judicial reform, without which local school districts will not have autonomy to operate their schools.

CHAPTER 11

Public Law 94-142

This federal legislation, passed in 1975, mandates equal educational opportunity for all handicapped children from ages six to 18. Disabilities covered include learning disabilities; hearing, visual, and orthopedic impairment; emotional disturbances and other physical conditions that impinge on optimal learning. In earlier times, these children may have been grouped in segregated classes or separate schools. This law presently requires that they be "mainstreamed," or integrated, into regular classes.

Special education requires more extensive funding, well above that budgeted based on the per-pupil expenditure allocated for regular classes. Parents of handicapped and learning-disabled children suffer no small amount of anguish and hopelessness in their efforts to nurture their children to independent and fully functioning adulthood. So, we celebrate allocation of federal monies that now make available educational programs tailored to the unique needs of handicapped children.

This new law, placing special education students in regular classrooms on a part-time basis, was acclaimed as a promising program whose time had come. As one of the greatest educational developments of the century, it represented undiluted democracy.[1]

Decisions about what needs to be done are easy. How to accomplish objectives is far more difficult and divisive. Public Law 94-142 mandates the role of the parent or guardian, as equal partners in making educational decisions. Educators sincerely desire parent involvement in the school program. But this law enables the parent to overrule administrative and curriculum decisions approved by the school principal and district Board of Education. Children deemed candidates for special education must have parental permission to be grouped in such classes. They must be evaluated by a team of professionals and tested in their own language. An *Individual Educational Program* (I.E.P) is required to be designed by a committee comprised of the parent, the special education teacher, a psychometrist, a regular classroom teacher and the principal or his designee. The parent makes the final decision, including what regular class into which the child is mainstreamed.[2]

Seymour Saranson, Professor Emeritus at the Institution for Social and Policy Studies at Yale University, presented conclusions about why educational reform is not attempted or is carried out in an educational context of which the reformers have little or no knowledge. In this connection, he referred to power relationships, power's unequal distribution, and how it is employed in implementing change. Saranson maintains that any effort to deal with or prevent a significant problem in a school system that is not based on reallocation of power—a discernible change in power relationships—is doomed. Public Law 94-142 changed the power relationship between parents and educational decision makers.[3]

Assignment of children to regular classrooms is generally done on a heterogeneous basis at each grade level. Each class includes students that reflect a wide range of achievement and ability—slow learners, average, above-average, and gifted learners. Ideally, the range of differences is kept to a minimum. Group teaching is the typical mode, but teachers seek to individualize instruction with such strategies as temporary subgroupings within the class, adjusting the pace of learning, leveling concepts and making individual homework assignments.

Nevertheless, this law allows parents to overrule the plan designed and recommended by the committee and elect to mainstream their children to a regular classroom where individualization is already stretched to the limit. When this happens, an inordinate amount of time is wasted or, at least, diverted from the regular program. Moreover, assigning a child with a learning disability to inappropriate coursework may cause the child even more frustration and create learning blocks that may deter later success.

A less restrictive environment may enhance learning. Children learn from each other, and the socialization process is highly valued. The typical school program offers a wide range of class assignments apart from self-contained special education classes; but decisions about class assignment and how instruction should take place must remain the prerogative of professional educators.

Equality—other than equality before the law—is a problematic and often pernicious social value. The celebration of equality of condition is merely envy tarted up in the clothing of compassion.[4]

Every child is precious and every educable child is entitled to equal opportunity to succeed in a public school. P.L. 94-142 is a noble effort to make this possible. Parents are encouraged to be involved in public school matters—particularly, with regard to what is taught. Issues about *how* instruction takes place require professional knowledge and training and should be addressed by professional educators with this expertise.

Rather than continuing the practice of mainstreaming, a practice that is incongruous to good instructional grouping practice, effort should be made to protect the mainstream of public education.

In 1978, three years after passage of this law, Ernest Boyer, then Commissioner of Education, reported that this Act had created fewer problems than school administrators and teachers had expected. No one knew how many handicapped children there were; and regular teachers were not believed to be ready for handicapped children. In addition, tight budgets would be stretched to provide the comprehensive services mandated by the Act. He felt that the regulations were fair, but if they needed change, "we would change them."[5]

Changes are needed.

CHAPTER 12

Illiteracy—
Our National Disgrace

Why are our children not learning to read? All children who are not physically or mentally handicapped can be taught to read if provided with appropriate learning conditions. Helping children and youth become functional readers to prepare for citizenship in a representative democracy is a high priority. In preschool and primary grades, they grow, learn, and mature at different rates. By fourth grade, they are expected to be proficient in independent reading for information and pleasure.

Among people with as much as 12 years of schooling, there is an ever-growing population of functional illiterates—people who cannot read training manuals, books, magazines, or product labels written above fourth- or fifth-grade level.

Students who leave school before graduating can be reliably identified because of reading failure at an early age. Despite the overload of information about this issue, one in four children still grow up as semiliterate or illiterate. Parents know that something is wrong and frequently point to the absence of "phonics" in the reading program.

Blaming the schools has become a national pastime, says David Harman. We blame them for strained race relations, productivity slippage, lack of work ethic, being behind in the space race, limited emphasis on science education—and deficient reading skills. He does not believe that illiteracy can be traced to a failure of the schools, but rather reflects dynamics of interlocking frameworks, and roles played by work places, and the media.[1]

There is enough blame to go around, but arguably, we must first look to the education establishment. Citizens expect professional educators, with training and experience, to use good judgment in selecting teaching materials, to use reliable teaching methods and work earnestly to teach all students to read. Children develop code-breaking skills at the preschool and first grade levels. They should become fluent readers during the second and third grades and, by the fourth grade, should be able to read for information and pleasure. Because illiteracy is interpreted so widely, it is acknowledged that simple decoding does not represent the true upper limits of reading, but children must pass through those initial stages to develop comprehending skills and find meaning from the written word.

During the 19th century students who were taught to read early using the phonics system were able to read classic literature as early as the fifth grade. The origin of the "look-say" readers can be traced to the work of Thomas H. Gallaudet, who, in 1835, developed a primer to teach deaf children who had no conception of spoken language or sound-symbol reading. Such books were adopted in the Boston primary schools. In 1839, teachers were being trained in the Normal Schools at Lexington, Massachusetts, to use this "whole-word" method to teach reading. It was not until 1844 that Boston schoolmasters rebelled against the "whole-word" method and restored the alphabet system.

The "whole-word" method was revived during the beginning of the progressive education movement led by John Dewey from his Laboratory School at the University of Chicago and Columbia University. Samuel Blumenfeld relates how, in

1955, Rudolf Flesch in his bombshell book, *Why Johnny Can't Read*, blames the "look-say" teaching method as the cause of reading failure in the schools. Despite the subsequent outcry from parents, no major publisher brought out a phonics-based basal reading textbook series until 1963. Nevertheless, 85 percent of primary schools were continuing to use "whole-word" reading programs.[2]

Extensive research by Dr. Jeanne Chall, professor of education at the Harvard School of Education, documented Flesch's charges against "whole-word" reading instruction. In her 1967 book, *Learning to Read: The Great Debate*, she concluded that the phonics, or code, approach produced better readers than the "whole-word" method. Ironically, the federal government continued to spend billions of dollars in support of sight-word reading methods that were used in the Right to Read, and Title I programs. Except for lining the pockets of textbook publishers, and creating new jobs, such federal programs are documented to have failed.[3]

The controversy over reading instruction still rages. Currently, it revolves around the superiority of phonics over the "whole language" approach, a system originating in Canada that has gained popularity in American public schools. It is described by E. D. Hirsch as a method based on the assumption that learning to read is analogous to the original, natural learning of the mother tongue. The child should be exposed to print in meaningful, life-like contexts and should be encouraged to figure out the oral written correspondences by the same sort of trial-and-error processes that characterized his or her learning of the mother tongue. Learning to read is to be understood as "a psycholinguistic guessing game." Of the research data on the two approaches— from experiments in laboratories, classrooms and clinics; from eye movement and language studies; and from practice and theory—most support the traditional-classic approach.[4] Leaders of the whole language movement make no secret of their contempt for phonics. Critics who push for phonic-based teaching are often derided as members of the "Christian Right" or educational simpletons. Mainline departments of psychology that have researched this matter, along with Jeanne Chall, support a middle-of-the-road approach: a combination of phonics and whole-language.[5]

It must be strongly stated that we should not rely only on appropriate textbooks and instructional materials. We expect teacher preparation programs in colleges and universities to train prospective teachers on how to teach reading effectively regardless of the available instructional materials. Ironically, most elementary teachers earn teaching certificates without gaining the knowledge and practice that would ensure they will, in fact, become good reading teachers. Related course-work serving to meet certification requirements includes orientation to fundamentals of teaching reading, methodology, recommended materials and children's literature. Such courses are fundamental, but may not actually translate into effective practice or desired outcomes.

As inclusive and complete as such curricula may seem, they may not incorporate demonstrations in teaching-directed reading lessons by the instructor or students under the guidance of and critique by the teacher. Such activities should include the range of understandings associated with a complete lesson plan, use of the publisher's textbook manual, and lesson evaluation. Although the teaching manual should be carefully followed, it does not take the place of an effective teacher, and it is assumed that good teachers will utilize a variety of supportive activities to reinforce the structure outlined in teaching manuals.

Internship, which begins later in classroom settings, provides real-time opportunity for mentors to nurture novice teachers in crystallizing effective teaching skills; otherwise they may later revert to practices they observed as elementary or secondary students. Care should be taken that, as interns carry out directed reading lessons in regular classrooms, they receive close observation and beneficial critique by the supervising instructor.

Insanity has been defined as doing the same thing *over and over again*, and expecting *different* results.[6] On the recommendations of textbook-selection committees, State Boards of Education *repeatedly* approve the latest basal reading programs. Touted as *the* panacea for solving reading problems, these books are frequently discarded after the book contract expires. This ongoing process only prolongs a condition that some describe as "the education dilemma of the century."

If members of state boards of education, who have responsibility for approving all textbooks, are made aware of reading research and background of basal reading materials, they are more likely to possess the knowledge necessary to authorize reading materials that will markedly reduce illiteracy in their states.

The variety of reading programs numbers in the hundreds and can be categorized in approximately ten approaches, from basic phonics and linguistics to "whole-word" and perceptual discrimination. The English language is not entirely phonetic, and it is acknowledged that teaching "phonics" in isolation is not desirable in contrast to more eclectic methods. But research in reading methods since the early 1950s points undeniably to the superiority of phonics-driven programs over all other methods. Because of the interrelation of the various language skills, the "whole language" method now in vogue enjoys widespread acceptance.

The success of the "whole language" method may well depend on the quality of teacher training and the "IF" factor:

- IF teachers understand the need for phonics,
- IF phonics remains the predominant component of the program, and
- IF teachers have sufficient skill to incorporate phonics in reading instruction.

CHAPTER 13

Say What?

"Man, I mean, like wow!"
"You know what I mean?"
"Did you ast (or ax) if you could come?"
"Om comin witcha."
"Jeet yet?" "No, jew?"
"Dat happen to me aulla time."

We wonder how students develop such speech habits during 12 years of public education and are astonished when they are awarded high school diplomas.

As important as learning to read is, our ability to communicate effectively is equally critical, and it should be taught in concert with reading because the other communication skills—listening, understanding, speaking, and writing—are integral.

Speaking is a powerful method of communication. It is the one we use most and is closely related to our ability to think. Unfortunately, the integrated way in which the several skills are taught in the typical "language arts" curriculum has resulted in insufficient stress on the speaking component. Learning to decode printed material does not automatically translate to ability to speak effectively; rather, planned, direct instruction in critical listening and formal speaking instruction is needed.[1]

English is taught and heard in all 12-grades in public schools. We scratch our heads at the realization that the majority of high school graduates are unable to use standard American-English pronunciation, speak in complete, grammatically correct sentences, or write a complete, correctly punctuated sentence. Home and family environment, neighborhood influence, peer pressure, minimal academic expectancy, and marginal instruction are some of the factors that can account for this, but the principal problem is that students are not hearing good speech and having it reinforced.

Why have we not attacked this problem with more vigor?

Children speak the way they hear others speak. Speech is a skill learned from influences in our social environment. Since children have mastered most of the basic grammatical fundamentals by the time they are four years of age, heredity and environment are strong factors in speech development. Children reared in affluent homes learn to speak more effectively than children from homes where parents are less educated. Although those factors are strong influences in speech development, more important are teachers, students' peers, the school atmosphere, and instructional practices.[2]

Students normally develop at least two sets of language habits that they use in keeping with a particular social situation. "Tho the ball," may be OK at a Little League game, but students know they are expected to say, "throw the ball" when making an oral report in class.

Parents, who take care to instill good speech habits in their children, are surprised when their children, around middle-school age, eagerly reach out for new bits of slang and unauthorized language from their friends and mass media.[3]

Fortunately, there has been a growing acceptance of the importance of oral language, referred to by the National Council of Teachers of English as "the only genuine form of language."

Words have meaning, but meanings change markedly depending on the way they are pronounced or mispronounced.

Effective communication is sorely hindered, for example, when diphthongs and digraphs are not articulated well, when consonants are not sounded (particularly at word endings) and when sentences are not complete and spoken grammatically correctly.

We should not wonder about the national furor over the belief that our children are not learning to read while instruction in speaking—our most used mode of communicating and on which we depend to think critically—is so neglected. It is an integral component of what it means to be literate and should be a continuous thread of a structured curriculum from preschool to the 12-grade. It is a goal we can achieve if speaking skills are specifically targeted and required in a carefully planned speech curriculum and integrated throughout the total school program. We have no control over speech children hear at home, in the community, or on television and radio, but we should tightly control what they hear at school.

Kindergarten and elementary grades include a wide variety of activities that require students to speak. Rather than list examples, it is simply recommended that a process of "shaping" be employed by teachers that obviously begins with modeling correct speech.

The school district should require that every professional person with whom students come in contact in either formal or informal settings should exemplify correct speech. All non-professional employees and support personnel should be expected to model correct speech as well.

A structured, formal curriculum should be put in place to include a wide range of settings that:

• Increase opportunity for students to speak and respond orally;
• Require teachers to follow a practice of "shaping and molding" student speech at all grade levels and in all subject areas; and
• Employ classroom testing programs to include a wide

variety of oral responses on "check-ups," and at the end of teaching units.

The school environment should be characterized by correctly spoken English. When schools focus enough effort to make this a reality, there will be greater probability that students will learn to speak correctly and effectively.

CHAPTER 14

Teacher Unions

The National Education Association is a formidable obstacle to reclaiming our schools. It once served to promote professionalism in teaching and in its nobility and excellence and to protect educators from the tyranny of political pressure or social intolerance. *Today's Education*, its official organ, offered informative articles in a range of educational content focusing on professional development and classroom instruction. By 1968, however, this organization voted for a series of actions designed to increase NEA's power to effect changes in the organized profession and in American society.

In the ensuing years, the NEA has grown into a political behemoth with power to control every aspect of public education in America. Presently among public school teachers, 72 percent are Democrats, 30 percent are Republicans, and 28 percent are reported to be Independents. Yet, 99 percent of NEA's political action funds go to political causes not supported by most members.

Once teachers resisted unionization. Teachers eventually turned to unions as a coalition for reform because of their powerless relationships with policymakers, low pay, lack of regard as professionals, and inability to effect change.[1]

The extent of control that teacher unions exert is seen in such actions as:

- The right to approve school board policies and administrative procedures *prior* to implementation;
- Control of teacher testing and evaluation procedures;
- Power to retain the teacher tenure law;
- Influence over curriculum content, and, most disturbing,
- Legal defense of *incompetent* teachers.

The power of unions to shape school policy is seen in the union's control over the structure of teachers' jobs, right down to the number of minutes of preparation time, lunch or hall duty, tutoring students, extracurricular activities, and anything else they might be asked to do.[2]

The NEA has almost 2.2 million members in 11,300 affiliates after its merger with the American Federation of Teachers. Approximately 80 percent of public school teachers are NEA members who pay about $750 million in dues from 13,000 school-district affiliates. Rank and file members are not always pleased with the way their dues are spent. Their continued membership is based primarily on the promise of legal protection against lawsuits, reassignment of teaching stations, and threat of termination.[3]

Legislative agendas formulated by the NEA each year and actively lobbied in Congress contain few provisions bearing on educational improvement or relating to the collective bargaining process. Rather, it spends its $750 million budget to influence legislation in such areas as school vouchers, censorship, gay rights, sale of school facilities, English as the primary language, affirmative action, and human rights.

Most common of parental complaints is that children are being taught by an incompetent incapable of uttering a grammatically correct sentence or, worse, someone habitually inebriated.[4]

The NEA will legally continue to operate as a union and continue to exercise collective bargaining, which it has been doing since 1966, when its legal right to do so was earned. Despite increased job security, higher pay and other economic successes by the unions, educational outcomes have not dramatically improved.[5] Because of NEA's political might and questionable goals, success in taking back our schools will not be realized unless we achieve a *balance of power* among school administrators, parents, and teacher unions.

Because unions make quality control of tenured teachers so difficult to enforce, we must focus our efforts on screening new teachers carefully before they achieve tenure. This is not the complete solution, but implementation of a strong supervisory program for probationary teachers must include more frequent classroom observations, personal counseling, compulsory continuing education classes, and regular progress reports by supervisors.

The recommendation for tenure status should include a satisfactory report from a school district Peer Review Committee in collaboration with the local school administrators. States and local school districts should establish, or reestablish, organizations for teachers and administrators at the several grade levels for professional growth, and to allow representation in system-wide planning.

Rather than the typical adversarial environment reflected at union-management bargaining tables, there should be fostered a partnership arrangement between teachers, administrators, and policy makers to insure teacher involvement in all areas of the school program. A key aspect of such an arrangement would be a guarantee of free legal assistance as long as approved Board policies are followed.

The balance of power that is needed may not be achieved without court intervention, not unlike the way teacher unions gained their inordinate power. Teachers are closer to parents on the power pyramid than is any other group. By united action, a coalition of parents and teachers can be a major force to accomplish needed changes. These are the two groups that have daily contact with children; they are directly responsible for an individual child's success. This should help overcome real and perceived barriers against their joining forces to work toward increased decision-making power in the schools.[6]

There is evidence that the NEA's leadership is out of step with its own membership. Ninety-one percent of teachers support higher graduation requirements, and greater emphasis on academic subjects; seventy-four percent favor increasing homework; eighty-seven percent favor career ladders, and support changes that would make it easier to remove incompetent teachers.

Teachers need to start defining the interests of their profession in more visionary terms and shed tendentious aspects of unionism.[7]

CHAPTER 15

In Loco Parentis

H istorically, American public schools have operated with the understanding that the school assumes the role of the parent during the time students are under supervision and control of the school. In recent times there have been lawsuits by civil rights and children's advocacy groups to eliminate or weaken this practice.

Parents expect that, from the time a child walks onto the school campus or steps on a school bus, provision for his general welfare is commensurate with what a parent might reasonably provide. The power of the school to maintain a civil, orderly learning environment is seriously eroded if *in loco parentis* is not legally observed. More than related to student accountability, it implies a school ethos characterized by nurture, shaping, and standards parents would provide.

Despite the long-standing practice of providing parenting oversight, schools have become more fearful of legal action from parents who allege that their child's "rights" have been violated. School administrators have become more reluctant to enforce student control measures due to uncertainty over what is legal, rather than what might be proper. Because they believe that the courts were demanding a more permissive atmosphere,[1] the obvious result has been that schools have become more permissive.

In 1973, the United Nations issued its Declaration of the Rights of the Child as the guiding principle of those responsible for the education of the child, and that responsibility lies with the parents. The United States Supreme Court has supported this right in numerous cases since 1925, when it upheld parents' rights and obligations to guide upbringing of their children over those of states.[2] Few would disagree with the soundness of the principle that guides these rulings, but controversy arises when such rulings are not applied judiciously. Legal cases tend to be resolved around the "reasonableness" of an action taken. Parents and the school administrators (who may also be parents) may not agree on what "reasonable" is.

A person reaches majority usually at ages 16 to 18 (it varies from state to state), but for most legal purposes, a person becomes an adult at age 21. Until a youngster reaches legal age, or until he marries, or begins to earn his own living, his parents are still responsible for his nurture and support. Although children are entitled to basic freedoms guaranteed by the United States Constitution, they do not enjoy precisely the same rights and privileges as do adult citizens. Does the Fourteenth Amendment allow students, even with approval of the school district, to draft a Student Bill of Rights that disallows discrimination between sexes with regard to school attire?

A youngster in a New Jersey school was caught smoking in a restroom. She had marijuana in her purse. The parents sued on grounds of illegal search and seizure. The case went to the Supreme Court. Fortunately, the school system prevailed on the basis of the argument that "school authorities act *in loco parentis* when parents entrust their children to the public schools." They maintained that to protect students school officials must provide an environment in which learning can take place. Continuing their argument, "to do so they must act in place of parents, and need broad powers of discipline and action, and there was reasonable cause for searching the student."[3]

Morrel Clute expressed an opposing point of view about this issue. He believes that children are citizens and, as citizens, have constitutional rights and cannot learn to become good citizens unless they can actually exercise those rights. He refers to the ruling by the Supreme Court in 1967: Gerald Gault, a 15-year-old youngster, was accused of making offensive phone calls. He was awarded all rights of adult suspects, but was given a more severe sentence than he might have if he had been an adult.[4]

A practice that subsequently followed, especially in urban school districts, was the codification of student "rights and responsibilities" into voluminous rulebooks. The chief sponsor of these changes was the ACLU. Their publication, "Academic Freedom in Secondary Schools," included suggested model procedural material for use in school districts. Their purpose was to replace what it called "rule by personality" of school officials (*in loco parentis*), with a "rule by law," that explicitly defined the extent and limit of adult authority.[5]

We should guard the autonomy of parents in matters related to the operation of their schools. School policies that bear on student life should be developed cooperatively with parents, reflect beliefs and standards of behavior acceptable to the school community, and set these forth in a student policy handbook. There should be clear understanding of procedures to be followed in matters that relate to student behavior, student attire, locker and book-bag searches, and the penalties that will be imposed.

Students need to learn democracy in schools through democratic experiences, but schools that allow students to follow majority rule foster arrogant selfishness and inconsiderateness in the name of democratic rights. In some quarters, support has been given to formulate "Student Bill of Rights" statements that include provisions that ignore parents' rights. Boards of

Education and school principals are well advised to maintain systematic procedures to elicit suggestions and recommendations from organized student groups. This promotes a continuing awareness of student concerns and problems and strengthens the role of student government in the school program. Moreover, it helps students to better understand the social and moral principle of balancing individual freedom with societal or group needs—the basis for the full range of school regulations and public law—that *rules and regulations are meant to protect, not just to punish.*

Bill Honig pointed to unfortunate trends that have plagued our schools since the 1970s. He said, "the schools need to stand up for a discipline policy that unequivocally puts the interest of the majority of conscientious students ahead of the disposition to misbehave of a few bad ones." In the absence of legislation for which they work, activist groups will continue to crusade for all kinds of "rights"—many of which seem absurd when examined legally and logically.[6]

CHAPTER 16

Parent Associations

P arent-Teacher Associations (PTAs), also called Parent-Teacher Organizations (PTOs) in some areas, operate with approval of the local district school board. They provide a mechanism for parent involvement, promote close relationships and understanding and facilitate general oversight of the total school program. These benefits are not realized when such groups are poorly administered or when they do not exist at all. Less obvious, but equally significant, rewards are enjoyed when a unifying process takes place within the attendance area as parents cooperate to achieve common goals and offer mutual support as they share childrearing concerns.

Parents welcome timely reports and want to ask questions about all aspects of the school program. Time should be routinely given to this at all meetings. Time must be allotted to discuss such matters as fund-raising projects, school beautification, and voluntary work in school offices and classrooms. However, it is proposed here that higher priority should be given to programs and activities that improve parenting skills and understanding of their child's total growth and development.

Most parent organizations do not function to benefit parents this way. Allen Small reported that, around the country, the mood regarding the PTA was characterized as indifference by parents as well as teachers. Typical meeting programs only remotely bear on educational issues. Musical talent is used to promote attendance; there was "hassle" over who volunteered to work at the upcoming fund-raising dinner, and the climax of business was attendance—the "room count."[1]

Historically, the family has been the first and primary influence in the education of children. We have no choice but to rely on the schools to provide aspects of knowledge and training that parents cannot provide, but the locus of responsibility remains on parents. Involvement in parent organizations provides an avenue for oversight and a participatory role in the child's education.

There is no lack of evidence that parent organizations are beneficial. In her research summary of more than 50 PTA groups, Melitta Cutright listed such advantageous outcomes as increased student achievement at all grade levels; she found that parents do not need to be well educated to be effective, and low socioeconomic students profited the most.[2] Such benefits were amplified in two reports published by the National Committee for Citizens in Education. Anne Henderson, staff writer for that organization, wrote that students in identical programs with actively involved parents perform dramatically better than those whose parents are not involved. Their research showed that schools closely related to their communities have better student bodies that outperform other schools.[3]

With knowledge of the importance of parent involvement, it is puzzling that more drastic measures are not taken to make parents active educational partners. But the schools are not law enforcement agencies. The appropriate option is to create and maintain viable parent organizations that provide information and skills that parents feel are beneficial to them.

A growing number of writers believe that lasting school reform will not happen without energetic parent involvement. Jill Bloom maintains that the level of parent activity in PTAs has not been enough to "turn the tide." She believes we need to move beyond the traditional image of the PTA to create real changes in our children's schools, and recommends more powerful and more effective action.[4]

There is no disagreement here. Parent power, collegial with insightful legislators and school administrators, is the coalition in which we should place our trust to "turn the tide." Our purpose here is focused solely on the role of the school to promote effective parenting skills.

Most school communities have many professional and non-professional resources to assist parents in this area. Included are persons available to make presentations at meetings or be available to study groups on a voluntary basis. Few parents of school-age children and youth have had formal training to become parents. They typically fall back on their own familial experiences or play it "by ear."

The school and the parent organization should cooperate actively to strengthen the education component in the operation of the parent organization, and thus, extend the influence of the school into the home in a meaningful way.

The end result should be improvement in school programs and improved quality of life in the local community.

CHAPTER 17

Shaping Student Behavior

A belief held for generations in rearing children is that "they learn by precept and example." They may well be taught to know right from wrong, and parents and teachers may take great care to demonstrate appropriate behavior, but the two axioms applied alone may not insure, or even make probable, desired behavior. As with a two-legged stool, a third leg is needed for it to serve its function and for the *precept and example* axiom to be credible, namely, a "shaping" component, best described as a potter shaping clay at his potter's wheel.

Psychologists refer to "shaping" as a process in which reinforcement is used to sculpt new responses or behaviors that were not previously exhibited and probably would not exist without outside intervention.

This principle is exemplified as parents warn children to tell the truth, help them understand the difference between right and wrong and point out the consequences of lying. Parents then serve as models of behavior (and character), when children observe that their parents are always truthful. This behavior, however, will probably not become integrated into the child's behavior without the continuing shaping process as the third essential component of the triad—reward for appropriate behavior and penalty for unacceptable behavior.

Teachers habitually fault parents and home environment for students' shortcomings. However, students spend almost half of their waking hours in classrooms or under the influence of the school. Edwin Frankel taught that we always have control over that which we *can* control.

Although teachers cannot control what happens in the home, they *can* and *should* have control over what happens in their classroom. Lack of awareness of "shaping" (continual intervention), how essential it is, and its absence as an integral part of the school curriculum may be linked to the widespread miscreant student behavior we see in schools today.

Teachers know the work of behavioral psychologists Edwin L. Thorndyke and B.F. Skinner, both pioneers in classical and operant conditioning. Unfortunately, most do not make it part of their teaching strategy because they lack training in the importance and application of shaping principles. Teachers must understand the shaping process and incorporate it in all their relationships with students. As the proverb reminds us:

The rod and reproof give wisdom,
but a child left to himself
bringeth his mother to shame.

When they feel that they have "done all the right things," parents are devastated to see their child, reared in affluence, given care and love, turn out to be less than a model citizen. As precious as infants seem to be, they are not born "good." Their knowledge of and subsequent goodness, along with all other desirable personal characteristics, are developed habitually in a process of shaping by parents and teachers.

Unfortunately, as stated elsewhere, there is unwarranted concern about student rights that causes school personnel to tolerate an inordinate level of student permissiveness, a factor that has had a debilitating influence in the development of self-direction in students, in school safety, and in the quality of instruction.

The application of shaping procedures is as important to the teaching act as it is in shaping behavior. Psychologist Daniel Neal recommends it as a useful way to conceptualize the teaching process, and teachers can utilize many situations to influence behavior by the conscious control of rewards and punishments.[1] The relation of discipline to effective learning is well established. Orderliness is obviously essential, but a shaping principle is observed when information is presented, modeled, and internalized in student responses and reflected in self-directed application of the concept.

The "spare the rod" proverb is more applicable for children too young to understand the danger of a hot stove. The subsequent punishment should be fully applied in a spirit of what has come to be accepted as "tough love." This should be part of the development of the child's conceptualization of the consequence of behavior.

Learning success is associated with classrooms that are well-organized, where students follow set routines, where class standards are reviewed frequently, and when students suffer restrictions and penalties for infractions of acceptable behavior.[2] We expect that public school employees who serve *in loco parentis* will hold to models of, and exemplify, good behavior, but these personality qualities may not be enough.

CHAPTER 18

Homework

Educational literature is replete with information about "homework" in research journals, textbooks, and in professional journals. We assume that homework is an important component of teacher training programs that include courses to help prospective teachers understand the purpose, value, and procedures that augment and extend the classroom into the home.

Good teachers consider homework an integral component in the total teaching process, and should continue to rely on homework experiences to achieve instructional objectives. So, it is more than a little disturbing to learn of the growing trend, notably in urban school districts, to reduce or eliminate homework assignments. Are teachers in those areas aware of the evidence of the positive relationship between student achievement and homework? Thoughtful school reformers are urging schools to assign more homework. Understandably teachers are frustrated when students refuse to do homework assignments. They accept the excuse that many students do not have adequate parent supervision after school, no space to do assignments at home, and such other excuses as unlimited television, extra-curricular activities, part-time jobs, and freedom to socialize on school nights. In earlier times, when children were better educated, they spent their evenings at home with parents or guardians doing homework, and free time was available only on weekends.

Teachers must stay aware and help parents understand that knowledge and information, to be remembered and to be useful, must be set in one's *long-term* memory. This requires that a process of internalization, or "clinching," must take place. The normal school day does not allow sufficient time to insure that important facts and understanding will be long remembered or applied. This is especially true of curriculum areas that require additional drill, review, and manipulative and repetitive activity for skill development.

Homework is essential to a complete and enriched instructional program. Bill Honig's observations spotlight the reasons homework is necessary and valuable, and they are based on sound research and experience. He reports that:

- Students can spend time on learning objectives beyond time allowed during regular class
- Assignments should require thinking, problem-solving, and self-testing
- There should be independent reading, writing, and composing reports
- Homework should be submitted on time to teach crucial lessons for later life
- Scientific principles can be conceptualized with simple kitchen counter experiments [1]

Parents should not be expected to teach material that should have been taught by the teacher. Students should have a clear understanding of the assignment's concept or operation to be done at home. Homework should primarily serve to reinforce prior learning by review, drill, research, related reading, and skill practice. Homework assignments are more meaningful if geared towards ability levels and particular interests of student groups. They need not be time-consuming and should serve a specific purpose.

Homework assignments are beneficial to teachers in assessing learning outcomes, revising lesson plans, adjusting the teaching pace and/or level of difficulty, incorporating more or less review and drill, and making decisions about reporting to parents. Obviously, this extends the teacher's workday and workload. Reports must be reviewed, assessed, graded, and data entered into gradebooks, but these chores can be somewhat minimized if student assignments are staggered.

As with other important components of school renewal, a sound homework philosophy should be spelled out in the school district handbook of administrative procedures and included as a part of the teacher's year-end evaluation.

CHAPTER 19

Bilingual Education

Legislation that requires non-English speaking students to be taught in their native language for the majority of the school day is having a crippling affect on children of immigrants.

Congress is not unknown for passing legislation to benefit special interest groups, and the Office of Education is not noted for always developing educationally sound regulations and guidelines; but it would be hard to cite a more egregious program than bilingual education. This issue began with the 1974 United States Supreme Court decision (*Lou v. Nichols*), in which it ruled that it was an unconstitutional denial of equal protection to provide only an English language education to non-English speaking students. The court did not prescribe a specific kind of bilingual program, but, due to conflicting views of ethnic activists, educators, citizens, and organizations such as LEAD (Learning English Advocates Drive), this issue has, as described by the *Washington Post*, become the single most controversial area in public education.[1]

The legislation was intended to help immigrant children learn English and make the transition into regular classes. Subsequent amendments added more restrictive requirements relative to student placement to ensure that respect for the child's own native culture was maintained. It is fraught with complaints alleging racism and segregation, and charges that the values of bilingual children were not being taught in the regular classes. The counterculture left and its allies, as referred to by Newt Gingrich, profess to smooth the path for immigrants through such programs that make it possible for children to continue in their own language, but this has actually made it more difficult. He recommends that immigrants make a sharp psychological break with the past and immerse themselves in the culture and economic system of the country that is going to be their home.[2] In the face of studies that reveal the student's ultimate command of English is weakened by bilingual curricula,[3] the counterculture left, labeled by Martin Gross as the "New Establishment," holds to the dogma that it is "psychologically repressive" to be forced to learn English. Bill Honig warns that, because America is an English-speaking country, adopting linguistic separation is an obvious problem. Our country was founded on the expectation that out of many traditions, one nation could be braided that would be stronger and more durable than any single strand.[4]

Foreign students can be taught in separate English classes until they develop sufficient English language skills to transfer to regular classes; they can be enrolled in both regular classes and English as a second language class; or they can remain indefinitely in classes taught in their native language. There are scholarly studies and journalistic exposes that reveal the fraudulence of bilingual education, but relentless political pressure from ethnic activists, particularly from parents whose children should most benefit, disallow any alternative other than full-time classes in the native language.

"Total-immersion" programs have proved to be more successful than bilingual classes. This approach allow students to be tutored by bilingual teachers while remaining in regular classes or assigned full-time to English classes taught by a bilingual teacher, which makes sense. Guidelines now allow for federal funds to be used this way and interest in this approach is increasing.

Bilingual legislation was well intended. Although classes were designed to be transitional, students frequently remain in such classes for many years. It was assumed that they could learn English in one lesson per day over a three-year period. Despite limited success, this politically motivated program is still in place. The fabric of America is beautified with swatches reflecting colors of all races and cultures, and sounds of different languages sewn together with English as the primary language. The "American melting pot" metaphor may allude best to a steeping pot used to blend diverse cultures into a common one, and there is no expectancy that the various colors not retain their identity or brightness. Freedom in America does not disallow the celebration of history, heritage, or continued use of one's language of origin. Immigrants have traditionally immersed themselves in English as they sought to build a new life for themselves and their children.

Non-English speaking students would be better served if states were allowed to use grant funds for self-contained, full-time English-speaking and writing classes designed to prepare students to transfer to regular classes within less than one year. This is not time lost; rather, it is a sacrifice that is required to achieve the long-term benefits of becoming fully functioning American citizens.

CHAPTER 20

The Pre-adolescent Puzzle

More than a few parents are perplexed in coping with their children's behavior as the youngsters fumble through the stages of pubescence and adolescence. Many teachers express the belief that, to work with kids at this stage of development, "you have to love them."

Pre-adolescents, ranging in age from 11 to 12 or 13, currently attend junior high schools or so-called "middle schools." Regardless of the title, such schools should be structured to meet the unique needs of this age group.

The middle school movement began during the 1960s as the result of awareness of the wide difference between children at ages 10 and 11, and between ages 13 and 14 or 15. (Because of the variability of human growth patterns, there is some overlapping.) Newly published research data described a body of growth and development knowledge, applicable to the special needs of these students in areas of physical, intellectual and emotional growth, which might serve to justify educational settings unique and apart from the traditional elementary and junior high schools.

Ironically, expansion of middle schools followed, but was based as much on such administrative concerns as overcrowding and facilitation of racial integration as on sound educational needs. Consequently, many new middle schools were not markedly different from the junior high schools they replaced.[1]

In contrast to pre-adolescents or pre-pubescents, characteristics of adolescents have been extensively studied and dramatized. The traditional view of human growth and development only in the three broad levels of *childhood*, *adolescence*, and *adulthood* may be, in part, responsible for the neglect. We perceive children's needs more clearly if we focus equal attention to later childhood and pre-adolescent stages of development. Middle schools that have emerged do not seem to be designed to accommodate the identified needs of this target group. Such characteristics, some of which are set forth below, cannot be emphasized enough, and should be considered for study and planning for appropriate middle-school programs.

Physical Development

Onset of puberty brings a quick end to stability and, from ages nine to 13, a sequence of changes takes place. Youngsters undergo an increase in height, body breadth and depth, heart size, lung capacity, and muscle strength.

- Kids are maturing at an earlier age, and display social interests earlier.
- They are taller, heavier, stronger, faster, more agile, and better coordinated.
- Myopia, associated with pubescence, is occurring at an earlier age.
- Teeth are erupting at an earlier age

Health and physical education programs should focus on developmental and remedial activities to develop strength, agility, speed, and coordination for all students. This is not the time for interscholastic sports. A group health curriculum, offered separately by sex, should include personal grooming, hygiene, drug abuse, family living, and other health topics deemed suitable for middle school students.[2]

Social Development

The school is a social system and serves as a family or peer group. It is an important agent to socialize and transmit culture. It has a subculture, a complex set of beliefs, values, traditions, and ways of thinking and behaving. There are pressures on pupils in:

- Learning to handle relationships with peers, parents, and teachers
- Integrating the simultaneous inconsistent demands of those groups
- Achieving a sense of autonomy and individuality
- Making sense of who and how valuable they are and developing a healthy self-concept[3]

The pubescent's view of his teachers, his sense of security and emotional support are all important factors in facilitating academic achievement. Some appropriate behaviors that are observed for this group are:

- Pair friendships with one's own sex
- Recognition that the opposite sex can be interesting
- Admiration and emulation of adult models, their views and ideals
- Enormous curiosity about the outside world, changing body responses, and a shifting sense of identity

Emotional Development

Concerns of middle-grade students do not focus on economic security, but do keep them from realizing themselves intellectually and socially. They worry more about the interpersonal demands they must deal with while striving to become autonomous and integrated persons. They want more empathy and open communication with parents, yet complain about lack of privacy. They want to be trusted, yet complain that teachers do not get to know them and show partiality. They worry about their popularity and fear their values may clash with those of their friends.

This is a period of self-doubt and anxiety as they try to decide what kind of adult they want to be.

- Should they take on the values of their parents?
- What will be their position in society?
- Their ideas of right and wrong are not yet crystallized.
- Latent interests are aroused.
- They have not yet learned to conform.[4]

Intellectual Needs

Intellectual growth occurs in sequential stages, but the sequence is invariant and is affected by genetics, experience, and culture. By the time youngsters reach the sixth or seventh grades, they should be ready to:

- Frame definitions
- Identify assumptions
- Deal with cause-and-effect relations
- Classify individual phenomena
- Generalize from recurring particulars
- Determine necessary and sufficient conditions for a conclusion

If the curricula are founded on an awareness of the nature of changing patterns of intellectual growth and their various needs, a more favorable learning environment is obtained[5]

Model Middle Schools

It is not intended that working drawings for a desirable program be included here. This should be a cut and fit process for the local school district. The goals of the middle schools harmonize with the objectives of elementary and high schools, except that the focus is on the unique growth and development needs of this category of children. However, the following selected generalizations might serve as a frame of reference for planning:

- Freedom of movement within a tightly structured school day
- Intellectually stimulating experiences within a variety of groups and settings
- Diagnostic services for planning individual programs
- Supplemental programmed materials for individual learning
- Non-graded arrangements for progress at different rates and depths in vertical and horizontal learning
- Developmental programs in reading/speaking as separate courses at all grade levels[6]

Middle School Teachers

Qualities of good teachers cut across all subject areas and grade levels, but the uniqueness of middle school students should justify specialized training for their teachers, as is required for children in primary grades.[7] Middle schools call for a special kind of teacher—one who is positive, personable, and sensitive to the special dimensions of the job. Emerging adolescents are developing their own values and self-identity, and the middle school's influence has a special and enduring importance. Middle school teachers are very much in the ethical business of "making men and women," as well as "schooling children."[8] Understanding preadolescents, who are groping their way from childhood to teenage years, should not be puzzling to well-prepared middle school teachers. The outward behavior these youngsters display belies their need to be handled with care. All good teachers should reflect caring behavior, but genuine love for middle school students is enhanced with a sound understanding in all areas of their total growth and development.

It is when students see evidence of genuine care for them that they reciprocate with respect and care for their teachers. Johann Von Goethe said it best:

"You only learn from those you love."

CHAPTER 21

Social Studies and
The Socializing Curriculum

If we accept the premise that the primary goal of our public schools is to prepare children and youth for citizenship in a representative democracy that is unique to America, we rely heavily on instruction in the social studies area to accomplish this.

The program of Social Studies in elementary schools currently includes a fusion of history, geography, and civics, with emphasis on man's interaction with his physical and social environment. Some critics have described this as a mishmash of social adjustment courses. The Social Studies program in middle and high school grades includes separate courses in civics, history, government, and economics. This arrangement fits neatly in a category of content described by Gail McCutcheon as a "patchwork curriculum."[1]

Weaknesses in this area of public school education are evident as we observe school "drop-outs" and high school graduates who demonstrate little knowledge or understanding of basic economics and our free-enterprise system, and reflect limited knowledge of world history and world geography. We are appalled by their ignorance of American history, our historical documents, the relationship of freedom to responsibility, and sacrifices that have been and must be continually made to preserve our freedom. Not the least of our fears is the current condition of moral permissiveness in America that is increasingly gaining acceptance. Admittedly, there are multiple influences at work that account for this, but we must point to flaws in the broad area of instruction we refer to as "social studies."

Jonathan Yardley laments that history textbooks are now instruments of social re-engineering. We have had dedicated, inspired teachers, but also some "steeped in the lunatic arcana of educational methodology." His accusing finger also points to textbooks that have become instruments of social and psychological reengineering. Rewriting the canon of American history, textbook publishers are agents of multiculturalism and self-esteem and avoid controversy that could hurt textbook sales.[2]

We don't know history because we have been taught—perhaps poorly taught—by teachers who hold only minor certification in history and struggle to stay one chapter ahead of the class. Added to the dilemma is the practice of using unqualified substitute teachers when regular teachers are absent. Approximately 20 percent of students leave high school before graduating and comprise a group that may be most in need of understanding American history, government, and economics. These courses are not normally taken before the last two years of high school. Exit examinations in vogue now do not normally test for knowledge and understanding in the aforementioned curriculum areas. New approaches to teaching social studies have emerged because of the work of Jerome Bruner. His theories hold that complex social studies principles can be taught at all levels, in keeping with students' cognitive development.[3] Thus, the broad band of social studies components can be offered conceptually to all students—simple in the beginning, and more complex at subsequent grade levels.

In light of shortcomings in the social studies curriculum, reform may be facilitated by incorporating the several disciplines into interdisciplinary strands, to be taught distinctly and continuously from kindergarten to the 12th grade. Component strands would include world, American, state and local history; American government and political science; economics; philosophy and psychology; sociology and anthropology; and history of religion. As we search for truth, we should be mindful that religion has been a major force in shaping the history of the world, and America in particular.

There is no more orderly way to handle the family of social studies than to have them "hang" on the single history thread that weaves continuously through all grade levels. We are aware of critics who believe that offering social studies in an historical context does not provide understanding and perspective; but good teachers make the past "come alive" by putting the present in historical context and helping students make valid assumptions and predictions about the future.

We should take care to protect the American social studies curriculum from revisionist influences such as those reflected in the recently published *National Standards* for teaching United States and world history. Martha Woodall notes that the reason for these new standards, formulated by historians, instructors, and curricular specialists, grew from the concern that Americans were not being educated to compete in a global economy. She reported that the "standards" have come under fire because the authors express unqualified admiration for people, places, and events that are "politically correct" and "much that is significant in our past will begin to disappear from our schools."[4]

We have witnessed notable developments in the social studies curriculum—restructuring by incorporating such disciplines as anthropology, psychology, and sociology, as well as remodeling the framework for organizing the curriculum on a conceptual base. But the area of social studies is not noted for explosive reforms, and they are welcome. The plea here is that we move from the era of the "patchwork curriculum" by developing specific teaching objectives for all social studies disciplines at each grade level and providing continuity by offering them uninterrupted through all the grades.

CHAPTER 22

Social Promotion and Grouping for Instruction

O f all complaints that citizens express about public schools, there seems to be unanimous agreement that what they perceive as "social promotion" should not be practiced. How clouded this issue is can be seen in reports of parents who sue school systems because their children have not learned anything. Conversely, parents want to sue because their children were not allowed to participate in graduation ceremonies, even though they have not completed requirements for the high school diploma.

Conventional wisdom in earlier times dictated that retaining students made little difference in learning achievement. However, it would be enlightening to have evidence indicating if this conclusion was based on retention in the *same* teacher's room with the *same* brand of instruction (repeating an obviously unsuccessful formula). The typical promotion policy in use allows students to be retained once in primary grades, once at the upper elementary level, and twice during the middle school grades.

Parents wring their hands today because they believe that students are passed from grade to grade, "given" passing grades, and learn very little in a "watered-down" educational program.

A survey released by the *National Assessment of Educational Progress* showed that eight percent of 17-year-old white students were functionally illiterate, as were a shocking 42 percent of black students. In 1977, a study by the College Board's blue ribbon panel pointed to the responsibility of the schools for the decline in *Scholastic Aptitude Test* (SAT) scores. They reported that there was no question about changes over the past 10 to 15 years in standards to which students at all levels of education are being held; absenteeism is condoned; letter grades mean less than they used to, and promotion from one grade to another had become automatic.[1]

Since much of the curriculum, such as mathematics, is sequential and builds on itself, it is critically important that students have a firm foundation at all levels of development. Passing a confused or ill-prepared student to the next level merely compounds the student's problem by causing a "learning block" that he may never overcome.[2] It also creates an impossible situation for the next teacher. "Promotion" should not be associated with reward; rather, it should be based on demonstrated achievement. Its primary function should be to assign students to groups in which they can most profit from the instruction offered.

Classification of students, assignment to classes, and promotion (or reassignment) to the next level of instruction by class, grade, or subject are major administrative decisions. Parental disdain for social promotion is justified because chronological age is not the most important criterion for grade placement.

Children in elementary schools are typically assigned to specific grade levels on the basis of reading achievement, along with consideration for level of maturity. In the face of criticism regarding social promotion, school administrators should be advised to carefully assess their approved promotion policies, along with practices that are actually followed. Although the policy itself might very well be adequate, it is often abused by well-intentioned teachers, principals, and parents or used as a vehicle to "throw away" students they consider to be unteachable.

State courses of study bulletins required by local districts already include learning objectives assigned by grade level and subject area. Basal textbooks that are adopted for use at specified grade levels offer additional learning outcomes. Adding more "benchmarks" to current state curriculum bulletins will probably not foster more effective teaching. However, if the specific learning outcomes are incorporated in state education department "teaching units" (as addressed elsewhere), grade level achievement can be more clearly differentiated and will make for greater accountability to a core curriculum.

Because of the marked variability of growth and development of children in primary grades, special grouping arrangements should be in place for regrouping as needed. When retention is indicated—when it is judged that a child will benefit from an additional year of maturation—it is wisely done as early as possible—ideally in the first grade. Subgrouping within classrooms provides a slower pace and opportunity for review and drill. "Side-bar" remedial programs should be a standard component of primary programs in elementary schools.

Assignment to the fourth grade traditionally has been made only for children who have developed sufficient reading skills to gain information and accommodate to fourth grade textbooks. All educable children should be well prepared to clear this major elementary school hurdle if they have been well taught. Children who may not profit from assignment to the fourth grade level should be carefully evaluated and considered for placement in alternative classes until they can later be accommodated in regular classrooms.

Students in many middle schools may be assigned alphabetically or homogeneously to the basic required courses. Some schools use test scores or past performance to place students in these core subjects. Despite protests from politically correct advocates, this practice is well founded, particularly for curricula sequenced by skill development.

The typical middle school promotion policy stipulates that students should not be retained more than twice, but, as stated elsewhere, chronological age and physical size may not be markedly important. A more important objective is achieved when middle school students are assigned to high schools only when they demonstrate high probability that they can succeed in the less structured and more rigorous curriculum and where their educational records will remain with them for the rest of their lives.

Depending on courses they select, students at the high school level tend to group themselves. In keeping with the message set forth in this essay, students learn better, and are generally taught better, when they are grouped homogeneously by interest and achievement level.

Mastery of coursework at the level set by the school district should be the determining factor in decisions concerning promotion and retention in secondary grades. Due to human variability, all will not realize equal benefits, but those who have not achieved an expected level of mastery should be required to repeat the course. This is a more desirable approach to school accountability than "social promotion" or offering easier, "dumbed-down" substitute courses.

CHAPTER 23

Neglected Dyslectics

For more than 30 years federal funds have been allocated for students who cannot be adequately accommodated in regular classes. They have been grouped in such special education classes as gifted, emotionally conflicted, hearing and/or visually impaired, and learning disabled. The process has been needed and beneficial. However, students who exhibit symptoms of dyslexia, except in a few states, have received little recognition and limited help.

According to the World Federation of Neurology, dyslexia is defined as a "disorder manifested by difficulty in learning to read, despite conventional instruction, adequate intelligence, and sociocultural opportunity. It is dependent upon fundamental cognitive disabilities which are frequently of constitutional origin."

Approximately five percent of children in the typical public elementary school are dyslexic. Few elementary teachers have the unique training or ability to identify as dyslexia the symptoms they demonstrate. Public Law 94-142 does not include provisions to treat them as a designated category of disabled learners because dyslexic children possess average to above-average ability. Thus, they suffer in regular classes, frequently drop out of school before completing high school, and go through life functioning and working as semi-literate citizens.

The number of students who suffer from some type of learning disability is estimated to be between eight and 15 percent of the school population. However, approximately three to eight percent have learning disabilities as the direct result of neuropsychological impairments. Dyslexic children fall into the latter group.[1]

The neurological impairment from which dyslexic children suffer is caused by limited blood flow into the angular gyrus, the area of the brain where language is processed. Auditory dyslexia is characterized by difficulty in integrating and processing what is heard, recalling sounds, and relating them to printed symbols.[2]

No cause for dyslexia has as yet been established, but brain mapping procedures and gene and chromosome research should provide clues. It is generally believed to be related to a genetic trait inherited from the father. Obviously, there is no medical cure, but with appropriate remediation, dyslexic children can become effective readers and fully functioning students.

Symptoms of dyslexia can be observed before formal schooling begins by parents and preschool teachers. This condition should be confirmed by a trained psychometrist or physician and remedial action should be taken before the end of the third grade.

The issue of dyslexia remains controversial. Despite the growing amount of neurological evidence, many critics do not accept the "label" or believe that it is a true learning disability. Parents, understandably, resist the notion that their child may be dyslexic. School administrators may not want to deal with an additional category of special education. Parents frequently believe that such problems lie in the fact that their child has not been properly taught how to read; and diagnosing dyslexia is still highly subjective. Because of the variability in growth and development of primary age children, observed symptoms of dyslexia may be due merely to late maturation.

Lori and Bill Grainger consider dyslexia part of a group of "trendy" terms like minimal brain damage and specific learning disabilities. This is because teachers have little idea of what dyslexia is, but they know they want to decrease their class size by shipping off their problem kids to be segregated in special education.[3]

Effort should be made to hold dyslexic children in the regular classroom, but provided with appropriate developmental remedial instruction. Temporary placement in the least advanced subgroup during the reading period may be most beneficial. Fortunately, there are commercial curriculum materials available for "side-bar" dyslexia classes, as well as materials and consultant help from non-profit organizations. The materials are developmental, highly structured, sequential, and have proven to be highly effective. These materials use phonics, not unlike the basal readers used in the regular classroom, but are more multi-sensory, with stress on sounds of letters, blending of letter combinations, and translation to writing. Surprisingly, such materials are recommended for use to strengthen and support all levels of achievement in the regular reading program.

An increasing number of states are considering legislation to incorporate special instruction for dyslexic children in their state program of studies. When teacher preparation programs incorporate a body of skill development to help teachers properly instruct dyslexic children, we may not need to continue referring to them as neglected.

PART SIX

Legal, Regulatory, and Administrative Bases For Renewal

CHAPTER 24

The Federal Government
and The New Plantation

The governance of public education in America has always been shared, not equally, by all levels of government—federal, state, and at the local level.

The men who framed our Constitution had divergent opinions about how and which children should be educated because some states already had provisions in their constitutions for education. Delegating of education to the states may have come about by default, but tradition and experience have shown the folly of a national school system, and the wisdom of allowing states to control public education. Fortunately, this arrangement has been continually reinforced in legal decisions and legal provisions; but the roles that the several governmental bodies should play is still clouded by constitutional provisions, legislation, court interpretations, and actual practice.

Most onerous is the role of the federal government.

No one should disagree that the federal government should maintain interest and be involved in public education. Article I, Section 8 of the Constitution charged the government with power to provide for the health, safety, security, and general welfare of the country. The interpretation of the "general welfare" clause has been controversial and seems to be the justification for the intrusion of the federal government into public education. But many believe that public schools are being used as instruments of social redemption, which heaps an extra burden on the schools. "When all else fails, turn to the schools," has become an habitual response to a social dilemma.[1]

Action by the federal government in the cause of public education is generally traced to the beginning of our country, when, in 1785, the Continental Congress set aside one section of every township for schools. This interest has continued over the years, with increasing legislation affecting schools. The increasing involvement and control of state education by the federal government are regarded by many as no less than dictatorship. The range of governmental agencies that oversee and administer state and local programs has grown steadily, justified by the assumed need to micro-manage and provide accountability for educational programs funded by federal monies. Following the Smith-Hughes Act in 1917, that provided an unending labor supply for factories in a burgeoning America, there have been continuous federally funded education programs, ranging from new vocational programs to child nutrition, disadvantaged students, to those whose primary language was other than English.[2]

The federal government's interest in public education is fundamental to our representative democracy. Such interest is directed particularly at health, safety, security, and general welfare of our country. In this regard, education in America should be a shared responsibility between the federal government, the states, and local school districts.[3]

The danger of federal control of public education cannot be overstated; but to abandon federally funded programs now in place is not realistic, and too costly to be underwritten by the states. During the Reagan administration, there was advocated the establishment of an educational foundation, independent of any cabine tlevel department that would end the flood of federal regulations and paperwork associated with federal aid to education.

It was intended to place primary decision-making power regarding use of federal monies for education in the hands of state and local school authorities. The President cannot end federal involvement in education by executive order, in isolation from the legislative and judicial branches of government, so, regulations that control operation of federally funded programs remain in place.[4]

The most recently approved "band-aid" reform, labeled "ed-flex," will allow states more flexibility to spend some of the federal funds without having to comply with every dot and tittle of the regulations. However, most regulations remain intact, a condition that may make no difference. Former Secretary of Education William Bennett recommends elimination of all red tape and would allow states to make contractual agreements in the use of federal monies. Funds from different programs could be combined and used in keeping with local needs and on the basis of local planning to achieve the purposes for which the funds were allocated. Accountability would be tied to documentation of improved student performance.

The extent of power, and manpower, in the Department of Education that administers and oversees federal funding for public schools is staggering. This agency, prior to its elevation to Cabinet status, provided a valuable service. It did not impinge on the day-to-day operations of the schools. It did not direct curriculum content, or how subject matter should be taught. Oblivious of the consequences, our Congress continues to approve more and more funds for the plethora of federal programs believed to cure or improve educational problems. Public pressure and limited resources for the targeted federal programs seem to account for the migration of states to the new Federal Plantation.

The subsequent increase in power of the Department of Education was justified on the assumed belief that education among the states would not be equal, and there would not be equal opportunity for all children within each state unless there was federal control.

The assignment of the Office of Education to Cabinet status need not be rescinded or abolished as some have advocated. Its role should be reviewed, however, to the end that its functions revert to the kind of resource services it heretofore provided.

We should not fault elected officials and others who work in the federal establishment for their efforts to "do good," however self-serving we might perceive them to be. What they believe about what should be done and how it should be done are assumptions that are not always well founded.

It is suggested here that any proposed solution to problems in education should provide for the maximum amount of freedom to be exercised at the school district level—more specifically, in neighborhood schools—and should be based on strategies proposed by the teachers, administrators, and citizens who support the schools. Congress should revisit legislation that affected elementary and secondary education since 1960, assessing its benefits and shortcomings, along with the regulations and injudicious application of civil rights laws that have a debilitating affect on the operation of our schools.

CHAPTER 25

The State Government and Limited Sovereignty

Constitutions of all 50 states include provisions to establish and maintain public school systems. They do not exercise complete sovereignty, as before the Civil War. States still retain the prerogative and freedom to renew public schools within restraints of federal executive orders, legislation, and judicial rulings. Such federal efforts have not focused on root causes of poor education or given proper attention to the largest group of public school youngsters—the "average." If states target this neglected majority, significant improvement of the total state program will be more probable.

Freedom has been aptly referred to as the "mainspring of human progress."[1] No progress will be made unless freedom, however limited, is protected. The intent here is to affirm the status of elected and appointed state officials and their sovereignty and power. They must exert *activist leadership*, rather than merely performing their duties in a routine, perfunctory way—as in an all-out war. Only then can we restore and renew public educational in a meaningful, substantial way and ensure the very survival of America.

CHAPTER 26

State Legislatures

State legislatures are the branches of government that exercise law-making power in the states. They pass tax laws, make appropriations, create agencies (such as county school boards) and corporate bodies, and perform other acts that do not violate state or federal restrictions. They have complete jurisdiction, control, and management of public schools in their states despite increasing encroachment by our federal government on public education.

This great power of this body is matched by the weight of responsibility it carries for its accountability to the quality of public education in each state. Reiterated in these reflections on public education is the belief that renewal will be achieved only by cooperative action—first by citizens, then primarily by governmental agencies with the necessary power and influence to effect needed change.

For years the federal government has mandated programs that have been politically motivated, have not focused on the most basic educational needs, and have not achieved the objectives for which they were begun. There has been a call for states to eliminate obsolete federal education programs and subsidies and redirect these funds to more appropriate uses. It is to the legislatures that American people look for leadership in determining state priorities and committing human and financial resources to meet urgent educational and economic needs.[1] Reference is made elsewhere to Diane Ravitch's concern that teachers are prone to be blamed for all public education's ills. She questions why the blame isn't shared by other agencies, such as the courts, media, federal government, universities, and state legislatures. Why pile on new requirements for such nonacademic courses as drug education, family life, consumer education, etc., while cutting away from science, math, history, and foreign language?[2] Legislators have little power over all such groups and influences, but they can exercise power to influence the quality of education in their states.

> *Legislation will not guarantee quality education,*
> *but quality education cannot be realized*
> *without good legislation.*

The power of elected representatives in our representative democracy flows from citizens who elect them; citizens have the power to influence their representatives. They share the power to take positive action equally as prime movers with legislators, governors, state boards of education, and local boards of education. Legislators typically maintain close contact with their constituents relative to their concerns, aspirations, and recommendations, and must take care to differentiate between the demands of self-serving interest groups and parents who seek genuine, sound legislation for the benefit of children. It is troubling to observe that legislators often seem to give the greatest attention to, and certainly seem to receive the most intense and constant pressure from, those well-financed organizations with the resources to wage strong lobby efforts for legislation that places their interests ahead of those of our children.

There is more than enough evidence of discontent, and certainly we know what the problems are. Research-based solutions are available and their merit should be debated for their soundness. The beauty and frustration of American democracy is that it is a participatory system. We elect our representatives to represent us—not their parties or special interest groups. They must act with courage and commitment to enact only the kind of legislation that will ensure meaningful and lasting renewal of public education in the states.

CHAPTER 27

The State Governor

The list of crises in America has ranged in recent years from the economy, poor leadership, moral issues, violence in cities, to the failure of schools to educate our children. Politicians who offer themselves for public office too often rely on polling data to find out what citizens are thinking and what they want done *at that moment*. They then, perhaps unwisely, base their actions on this information.

Regardless of ideology—liberal, conservative, or other—Americans agree on many issues, and they agree that education is a priority, surpassed only by the economy and lack of leadership.[1]

Unfortunately, agreeing on what our problems and priorities are is far easier than getting consensus on the proper course of action to solve them. Americans seldom agree on how problems should be solved. This is understandable. They may be caught up in the various problems, observing them firsthand, but have limited bases on which to formulate sound solutions. Their information may come from the mass media or special interest groups and may not provide the insight and full range of alternative measures, history, cost, feasibility, and probable consequences of each measure. Thus, the governor and other elected officials should be wary of structuring campaign platforms and making promises based only on polling data.

The governor can exert profound influence on public education. Analogous to the role of a football coach, he can set goals, recruit good players, provide expert training, formulate game plans, and call plays that could win the game. His philosophy, enthusiasm, and commitment should be reflected in all team members.

The power of the governor is seen in oversight of state expenditures, his influence over legislation, the appointments he makes, and service on boards and commissions that affect education. He can mold educational policy and oversee the implementation of the state educational program.

Judicious leadership is essential, but caution should be exercised to ensure that the several entities of state government that deal with education share his stated goals and, as important, the methodology envisioned to accomplish the goals.

Pitfalls of politically motivated, novelty, wasteful, or ill-conceived programs should and can be avoided if the governor is apprised of sound information, practices, and procedures that drive good educational programs, and then utilizes them effectively.

"Democratic governance," described as the body of elected officials who administer public education on school boards and district offices, are criticized for their bureaucratic nature—the main obstacle to school reform. Decisions are made at the "top," and those at the bottom are overburdened with regulations and choked with paperwork.[2] It is argued that this condition was not brought on entirely within the school community; but it has contributed to the failure of public schools to renew themselves—the prominent message in this book.

The power and influence of the governor, during his tenure, is such that he can begin the process of reform in key areas of legislation, policy development, professional preparation, certification, and evaluation.

We consider education an investment in children, but, equally critical, there is need to consider the investment in the educational personnel that make education possible.

CHAPTER 28

The State School Board

The power of state school boards, which operate in most states, is seen in their authority to exercise general control and supervision of the total public education program. The force of their policies and regulations, and oversight in the administration of their policies, shapes the design and quality of public education in their states. No aspect of public education is beyond their purview.

A long held belief that "schools belong to the people" is underscored as such legal bodies of laypersons exercise authority to formulate policies that shape the total structure of a state educational system. Professional educators are not prohibited from serving on these boards, but laypersons offer less biased views as they voice concerns, aspirations, and recommendations from citizens in districts that they represent.

Regardless of the varying sizes of the boards, elected or appointed, they should provide continuing attention to long range planning, coordination, and assessment of education in their states.

It is needful to point out that most educational reform efforts since the 1960s have been initiated by the federal government rather than by the states. Those educational "fixes" put in place by the states, since the early 1970s, typically focus on student achievement—promotion, graduation requirements, and competency testing. In their 1987 publication, *Results in Education*, the National Governors' Association members reported that they were not yet satisfied with the quality of education in their states. Earlier initiatives focused on raising performance standards, but steps taken had not completed the education improvement task. They believed that states should assume larger responsibilities for setting goals and defining outcome standards and stimulate local intervention.[1]

Reform measures continue to target "outcomes" rather than so-called "inputs." Many influences impinge on, and mitigate successful educational reform, but initiatives that focus on the development of professional educators should demand our highest priority. We should not take pride in the fact that the federal government, aside from politics, has provided educational services to children because the states have neglected to do so.

Power to effect significant change does not rest solely with state boards; rather, it is shared in varying proportions with multiple layers of entities—legislatures, governors, state and local departments of education, state and local superintendents, and, of course, citizens. But the state board of education should exert prime-mover influence to promote legislation and implementation of reforms that will more probably result in significant, appropriate, and lasting school improvement.

CHAPTER 29

The State Department
of Education

This department of state government, under the direction of the State Superintendent of Education or Chief State School Officer, executes policies authorized by the State Board of Education. Its major functions are generally classified as:

- Leadership for research, planning, advising, and consulting with federal, state, and local governmental bodies;
- Regulatory, to ensure appropriate use of allocated funds, implementation of laws, and appropriate practices and procedures; and
- Oversight for the general welfare of the state educational program.

By virtue of legal obligations assigned to him by the State Board of Education, the State Superintendent of Education has broad leadership prerogative to make positive, far-reaching reforms as he administers the day-to-day operations of the State Department of Education. He is required to stay active in budget planning, school construction, enforcing federal and state education laws, overseeing the myriad of reports from local school districts, and relating actively with the governor and other appropriate state agencies involved in educational matters.

The intent here is limited to discussion of topics that deal directly with the curriculum—the essence of this book—how curriculum is offered, how teaching should take place, and that good teaching, in fact, is taking place. Little change is probable without critical attention to this triad of concerns.

Education, as heretofore affirmed, is assumed to be a function of the several states. We hold states responsible, of course, but the actual process of educating children and youth takes place in school districts within each state, and in neighborhoods within local school districts. Our intuition and instincts tell us that our schools are more productively administered at the lowest practical level of operation. But, with more and more autonomy taken from local school districts, we have been delivered of unaccountable bureaucrats who believe they can micromanage our schools from afar. No engineering recommendations and no detailed drawings are offered here; rather, the objective is to point to remodeling needs within the existing state educational framework, and suggest the usual schematic from which planning can take place.

By virtue of legal obligations assigned to the Superintendent, along with broad leadership prerogative, he has leverage to effect positive, far-reaching changes. Selected areas that constitute the essence of this book relate to what is taught, how it is taught, and that it is effectively taught. Little change in public education will come about without balanced attention to this triad of needs.

Curriculum content. What our schools should teach has traditionally been the purview of citizens. The placement and sequence of information, and the teaching performance, has been the responsibility of professional educators. The body of knowledge that shapes the framework of public education increasingly grows and requires important decisions about what to revise, add, and delete. Course of Study Committees appointed by the State Superintendent meet regularly to recommend such revisions. Recently published courses of study bulletins include improved usability, with a wider range of knowledge strands, along with broad learning objectives. Teachers are encouraged to enrich the materials and add additional learning objectives unique to their local communities.

Membership on Courses of Study, and textbook Committees is typically composed primarily of professional educators who make recommendations about curriculum content and sequence for their grade level and subject areas. There is need to expand both committees to include lay citizens whose role would be to reflect cultural, moral, patriotic and ecumenically religious values that have provided order and meaning to life in our nation.

Teaching methodology. Although variation within the human species has emerged over time, there is no valid documentation that human physiology has basically changed Contrary to evolutionist theories, the way our brains function has remained unchanged. We have, and continue to amass information about how we learn, and how behavioral change comes about. Such data make up a body of learning principles that justify teaching as a valid profession—not unlike the body of medical literature that qualifies physicians as professionals Extensive educational research has shown that, when a specific learning principle is applied, a specific outcome will probably result. While the medical profession requires a specific procedure to be followed in performing a specific operation, teachers have freedom to preside in classrooms with complete disregard for the application of proven learning principles, without which effective learning rarely takes place.

Along with responsibility for approving curriculum content—namely, what is taught—it follows that the State Department of Education should maintain oversight over teaching methodology—how content is taught—in the way that medical procedures used by physicians are controlled by medical boards.

Teaching competence begins with knowledge of sound learning principles and understanding of how children grow and develop. Guided practice, under supervision of skilled professionals, is needed for teachers to internalize and appropriately use correct methodology.

Immediate oversight of school operations is best done in school districts—and, to the extent feasible, in local schools. It is not recommended nor is it practical for ongoing supervision be done by state personnel. It is recommended, however, that provision be made for a permanent team of specially trained professionals, as an integral component of the state departments, whose mission would be to strengthen the role of state departments in instructional leadership. (This objective is addressed in the chapter on teacher certification.) The team should be charged with providing closer oversight of teacher education programs in colleges and universities, ensuring that prospective teachers not merely memorize methodology information, but demonstrate mastery of its performance—showing clearly that it is part and parcel of acceptable teaching behavior that they will bring to the classroom. A second and equally important responsibility should be to hold scheduled continuing education clinics in designated regions of the states. Such programs should be targeted to personnel who have responsibility for local inservice training programs, instructional supervision, and other personnel who are responsible for instructional leadership and accountability in school districts.

Evaluation of teachers. There is no more effective and logical way to measure teaching skill than on the basis of the body of procedures and methodology approved by the teaching profession. Because the teaching act and measurement of the effectiveness of the teaching act are integral, clinics held by the state leadership team should also include training local district personnel to recognize appropriate application of sound methodology, as well as supervisory techniques to help teachers improve.

The responsibility for teacher evaluation, a quality control measure, is expected by citizens and should be honored by all school personnel. This obligation flows from the state department, and power is balanced when this process takes place in school districts. Power at the state level is energized when the kind of leadership, as set forth here, is exerted.

Evaluation forms and procedures are prepared by school districts and vary, so there is variance of criteria on which teachers are assessed. It may be misguided for the state to mandate a single evaluation form, but it is suggested that the state provide a model form and procedures from which local districts can create their own unique instrument that would include essential criteria to standardize evaluations throughout the state.

Essential components of a model instrument should include such criteria as knowledge of subject matter, use of appropriate methodology, classroom administration, effective use of time, and assessment of student learning. Local school districts would want to include a range of other items beyond those listed on the state model. Based on experience of teacher assessment practices in local districts, improvements and revisions could be incorporated and shared by the several school districts; however, basic standards of teacher performance set forth in state guidelines, as a vital accountability measure, should be maintained.

Certification of Teachers. The current practice of awarding teaching certificates, noted earlier, probably serves most to undermine efforts to improve public education. Many colleges and universities prepare excellent teachers, but the quality of teacher preparation varies markedly from school to school. Awarding teacher certification merely on the basis of transcripts and credentials from the training institution should not continue. Approval for colleges to offer teacher training is generally based on written reports related to courses of study paper qualification of instructors, physical facilities, and school organization. On-site visitation by state department inspectors may be mandated, but such visits are infrequent, cursory, less than productive, and do not guarantee effective teacher training.

Credentials may also not guarantee that teachers have been well trained or that they will be good teachers. Ed Hirsch recommends that concrete steps be taken in education schools to become part of the solution rather than part of the problem of teacher certification. He proposes that teacher certification be dependent upon prospective teachers' demonstrating adequate probing knowledge of the subject matters they will be called upon to teach, as well as adequate knowledge of mainstream research into the most effective pedagogy for imparting those subject matters.[1] By all indicators—whether objective data or first-hand observation—the intellectual caliber of public school teachers in the United States is shockingly low, and declining.[2]

Problems associated with teacher certification could be alleviated by the activation of a State Leadership Team, here-to-fore suggested, to include the following tasks as part of its assigned obligations:

- Schedule regular, extended visits to universities that train teachers to review the usual required written reports, but also to interview faculty and students, observe classroom instruction, review curriculum materials in use, and draw conclusions about the over all program quality. The leadership team would formulate critique data that would include commendations and recommendations for needed change.
- Prepare reports of "follow-up" data based on surveys of non-tenured teachers by universities where they were trained. Include recommendations for improving teacher training from supervisory and administrative personnel in school systems where non-tenured teachers are employed, as well as from the non-tenured

teachers themselves.

- Initiate collegial action among the governor, state department of education, legislature, and state judiciary, to put in place a board of state education examiners. As does a state medical examination board, which protects the health of citizens in the state, a state board of examiners would serve to preserve a measure of quality in public education in the state. A satisfactory score on a competency test would be required to earn certification. In 1990, 44 states were reported to have this requirement in place. The National Education Association would enhance its image as a professional organization and its standing with American citizens if it endorsed and promoted certification tests in all states.

Until needed reforms are made, state departments may have no choice but to continue to approve "baccalaureate degree" teachers (who have no pedagogy training), "out-of-field" teachers, and salary schedules that do not attract outstanding teaching prospects.

We will not have the schools we want until we take firm, resolute steps to deal with thorny problems that require courageous decisions. Teacher certification is a prominent one. The process of awarding teacher credentials should be considered as a narrow gateway through which only qualified teachers should be allowed to pass.

CHAPTER 30

The School District
Board of Education

The local school board is legally empowered by its state legislature to administer public education in each geographical district.

It is understood that public education is controlled by the several states; however, Hawaii is the only state that administers its schools at the state level. Policies and regulations in all other states are set at the state level, but the actual administration of schools is delegated to local districts with legal authority to implement state policies and regulations.

The importance of local school boards cannot be overestimated. The belief that education in America should be controlled in local communities is historical. Within the entire legal structure, education takes place at the local level. We should guard against any effort to usurp from local boards the wide discretionary power they enjoy within specific federal and state limitations. Lay citizens who are elected to serve as board members can best represent their neighbors and can directly control and influence the quality of education in their districts.

Public education is best served when the most capable citizens in the community offer themselves for board membership.

Sadly, this does not always happen. Board members seldom have time to learn the nuances of the job—and depend on the superintendent for information they should use to challenge him. Moreover, most board members do not view their role as representing the public; rather, they speak for the superintendent to the public.[1]

It can be argued that board priorities are decided more by personal politics, social concerns, and other self-serving interests than by educational needs. It is further suggested that confused priorities, community cross-pressures, stale methods, diverse student population, and unmotivated and poorly trained staff severely complicate the process of educational improvement.[2]

Donald Nugent reported the caustic criticism of the schools in his statement that, "the greatest single obstacle to a revamping of education in this country lies in the fact that the control and financing of schools is in the hands of thousands of local boards.[3]

Local boards may be the "sleeping giants" that we must awaken to achieve real school reform. Efforts to improve education have been advanced from outside agencies such as the federal government, private and commercial interests that market instructional materials and equipment. It is puzzling that the untapped power and influence legally delegated to local boards is not used. It appears that the power of boards is more frequently brought to bear to *prevent* school reform. They have not played a major role in deciding for innovative reforms.[4]

No small amount of distress, and stress, is caused by assigning, or accepting a job one is not prepared to do. School board members offer themselves for service because they want to improve conditions, but they do not always know the job requirements. Materials provided by the state Department of Education and the state School Board Association should be considered primary sources of help. The superintendent and his staff should provide in-service programs for board members on continuing basis. They should be acquainted with the history of public education in the nation, state, and the local school district; board policies and administrative procedures should be reviewed; and they should be made knowledgeable of federal, state, and local laws that circumscribe their legal power in educational matters.

Of course, members have no authority beyond that which they exert as a unified body, but their influence as individuals can be significant in promoting school improvement if their views and recommendations are soundly conceived. Membership and active involvement in the National School Boards Association provides powerful linkage to other school boards within the states and throughout the nation. Publications by this organization, as well as bulletins and research reports that should be provided by the local superintendent, are sources of great help to improve ability and understanding to deal with complex educational matters.

When board members are aware of vital issues, trends, failed programs, where programs are working successfully, and sound principles that make for successful programs, they can marshal power to play their appropriate role in school reform.

District school boards are charged by states and localities to make policy and govern local public education. Their willingness and capacity to lead, in large measure, will determine the long-range success or failure of school improvement efforts.[4]

The Educational Delivery System

There is a legion of support personnel whose services are essential to the operation of public schools, such as: bus drivers, maintenance workers, clerical staff, counselors, principal's assistants, and a range of workers assigned to the system's administrative offices. The quality of instruction however, will be measured by the efforts of *the district superintendent, school principals, and classroom teachers*—the delivery team. This triad of key professionals should serve to marshal all the school's resources and create classroom environments best suitable for effective learning. Any reform effort initiated from without the education establishment, to be successful, must focus on the roles of this category of personnel. Successful reform efforts, initiated from within the school setting will probably be credited to this group.

The District Superintendent

The power of the district superintendent to bring about school reform is enormous. Arguably, the most important decision the board can make is the appointment of its superintendent. Some advocate he be most knowledgeable in business and finance, but the point of view here is that, along with aforementioned qualities, he bring to the position leadership skills in the broad areas of teaching and learning.

Commitment to quality staffing should be reflected in board approved procedures for recruiting and hiring teachers. In the absence of a state test for the teaching certificate, there should be screening at the district level. As a branch of the state government, this practice is applicable within the jurisdiction of the local school board. Components of the test should include objective and subjective knowledge of the major and minor subject areas in which the teacher might be placed; human growth and development understandings and learning principles; and classroom organization. Communication skills should be assessed in an interview with a standing committee appointed by the superintendent. Implementation of this practice, along with character references, and review of teacher preparation credentials, should greatly improve the probability of learning success in the school district.

The superintendent walks a "tight rope" as he serves as executive officer of his board to enforce federal, state, and local laws bearing on public education, as well as numerous board policies. His philosophy, courage, commitment, and leadership skills can produce positive results despite legal, political and special interest influences that mitigate educational reform. The environment he creates and maintains should reflect a strong force to ensure accountability on all fronts, but in a climate where all personnel, particularly instructional personnel, feel secure and fully involved in the process of instructional improvement.

Because of his varied and extensive responsibilities, even in small school districts, he cannot personally make all decisions. But, he can take care that all administrative decisions primarily reflect the needs of the instructional program. His staff should include the most able person available on whom he can rely for advice and council in the broad areas of curriculum, teaching methodology, supervision of instruction, teacher assessment, and in-service training for teachers. Other staff members who assist the superintendent should be equally well trained. Their leadership is critical if the school district expects to achieve and maintain a high level of educational quality. Thus, their appointments should be based on experience, training, and ability rather than friendship, ethnic background, sex, religion, or any other reason merely to be seen as "politically correct."

The School Principal

Parents view the principal as the one most responsible for quality control of education in their neighborhood school, but his myriad duties mirror many responsibilities that the superintendent has. (Thus, a case is made here for a professional assistant in secondary schools to be assigned to work in the general area of teaching and learning on a full-time basis.) Teaching and learning is the purpose of the schools and should receive highest priority. The local school should have a scope and sequence of core subject matter for language, mathematics, science, and social studies for each grade level. If such material is not provided by the district school board it can be prepared from broad goals and objectives included in state course of study bulletins that are schematic in nature. State bulletins can be used to guide the formulation of teaching units that become "working drawings" to reflect more detailed and specific learning objectives for use in local classrooms. A basic standardized instructional program can be achieved with the use of such printed teaching units that cover the usual nine-week reporting period. Essential components of such teaching units should include: specific knowledge and skills to be taught, appropriate methodology and suggested activities, equipment and materials needed, and evaluation measures to determine what students have learned.

Advantages in utilizing standard teaching units are numerous. Primarily, they provide a control mechanism to assure delivery of a basic instructional program. Moreover, they serve as an accountability measure to the benefit of teachers in the evaluation process. Teachers should be accorded freedom to plan their activities to accommodate student achievement and ability; to enrich, and expand the units beyond the required objectives, and bring to the teaching act their individual creativity and personality. Other important improvements accrue in such areas as: curriculum revision, upgrading lesson plans, and upgrading equipment and materials. When standard teaching units are used, they provide clearer focus in the supervision of classroom instruction, more valid teacher evaluation and more realistic planing for in-service training.

Classroom visitation by the principal, or his designee, is an essential component of his leadership to assure quality instruction. As opposed to being perceived as "inspection," it should be considered by the entire school staff as a continuing improvement process. Criteria set forth on the approved Teacher Evaluation form should be the primary focus of a classroom observation. It is important that teachers know that the principal has the necessary training and skill to assess classroom activities, and they should respect his judgment. When teachers share in formulating conclusions about a classroom observation, and are involved in strategies needed to effect improvements, they are more likely to actively take steps to improve.

Classroom Teachers

The importance of the teacher's role in the delivery of education directly to children and youth is incalculable. He exercises delegated authority that flows through all layers of public education governance—from parents, state legislatures and state and local boards of education. The core, or basic, curriculum that should be required has been heretofore addressed. However, it is needful to remind that the process and methodology that teachers employ should reside as their prerogative— and should be defended—as long as the methodology reflects sound learning principles and appropriate application of understanding in the area of human growth and development.

Teachers should be paid commensurate with the noble role they play in our society, but money is not the only need. They should be freed from superfluous and meaningless reports and paperwork. Communities that regard teachers as professionals are apt to find themselves with teachers who act like they are professionals; but if communities treat teachers as sluggish, selfish government employees, they will get the kind of teachers they deserve.[5]

PART SEVEN

Conclusion

CHAPTER 31

Our Last Hope

We recall vividly the warning in the 1983 *Nation at Risk* report by the National Commission on Excellence in Education, paraphrased, "We would view as an act of war if a foreign power imposed on us our mediocre educational performance." We still faintly hear "cries from the wilderness" by such noted educational critics as Mortimer Adler, Jacques Barzun, John Goodlad, Ivan Illich and Hyman Rickover. A host of commissions, leadership consortiums, educational networks, and numerous educational summits have been dedicated to actively promoting improved education. Reforms put in place in so-called "silver lining" schools frequently produce only temporary benefits.

As we are wont to plead, "If we can send men to the moon, or send a mobile camera to Mars, why can't we build the kind of schools we need and want?" In truth, we have succeeded in space because of what our public schools used to be. The American people have simply allowed educational policy and ownership of our schools to be usurped from our control—foremost, by the federal government and, to a lesser degree, by teachers unions and self-serving political groups. Some advocates of school reform describe what is needed in terms of revolution, war, and the Marshall Plan. Arguably, we should muster such fervor and commitment to whatever measures we take.

Underscored again is the warning that we not completely abandon public schools. Their solid framework is still in place. The needed remodeling should be done only to the inside.

We are advised to give up on public education, free the schools from the clutches of the state and design a new system based on parental "choice" that would remove the top-down educational bureaucracy, introduce competition, and restore bottom-up control of public education. Families would then have a sense of "owning" the schools [1]

Private schools do better to some extent because they serve a select population group; they do better because they are free to put in place those attributes that characterize good schools. They are certainly locally controlled, and parents do feel a sense of ownership. Those who now crusade for charter and voucher schools may be shocked into reality when those schools become shackled with the kind of federal and state regulations that have kept public schools from evolving to what they should be.

By now, one can see that the essence of this book is reflected in its title. Choice is certainly advocated—not to abandon public schools, but to work to install renewal machinery that will help them become the kind of schools we need.

We see glimpses of public schools that are achieving very well. They are found in affluent neighborhoods, in impoverished inner city neighborhoods, and some mostly white and others with largely minority student bodies. Their success is not due to funding or religious affiliation; it is due to unique qualities and commitments they share in common. In contrast, only weak and nonexistent research data support educationalist fads and pseudo-reforms.[2]

Fortunately, there is *not* "nothing we can do." We have much consistent research about effective schools in numerous studies from the early 1980s. One notable example of such impact studies is a 1981 report by sociologist James Coleman that, in contrast to his earlier study, found schools *do* make a difference. He provided a body of evidence to demonstrate that school policy affects student achievement and behavior and cautioned school officials and policymakers to reexamine their curricula, policies, and programs.[3] The findings in the Coleman report, along with findings from other studies during the 1980s, became known as "effective schools research." This cluster of studies composes the most important body of educational information developed in the past two decades. Dr. Glen Robinson's summary of essential instructional ingredients was published by the Educational Reasearch Service in 1985.[4] Taken altogether, this great body of instructional research, could have served and should yet serve greatly to reform public school education.

Unfortunately, we have lacked leadership to engineer and implement what we know about what makes good schools—which, as history continually shows, must take place from within the educational establishment—by prime movers. A truism, applicable here, relates to the resulting atrophy and deterioration in the absence of continual renewal.

There are few regulations that discourage status leaders within school districts to engineer data from "Effective Schools" research. Schools should reflect clear goals, rigorous academic standards, order and discipline, homework, strong leadership by the principal, teacher participation in decision-making, parent support and cooperation and high expectations for student performance. There should be no excuse for not infusing in all classrooms the array of instructional practices and procedures compiled in the Rosenshine report, cited above.

As a detour sign placed at a fork in the road by a thoughtless prankster, the route of public education was diverted from its steady renewal journey, away from control of state and local communities it traditionally served. We should incorporate what has been learned from recent experience, to revisit, and begin again from the site of the detour. We should return to the path not taken with courage and revolutionary zeal—with total marshalling of our nation's human and material resources, not unlike that needed in the event military action is taken against us by a foreign power. Knowledge does not always motivate people to action. Fear always does.

The challenge to marshal and focus needed resources probably cannot be accomplished without the vision and determined action of "prime-movers," the kind of persons Alexis Carrel had in mind. He said that humanity has never gained anything from the efforts of the crowd. It is driven onward by the passion of a few abnormal individuals, by the flame of their intelligence, by their ideal of science, of charity, and of beauty. Such attributes are now needed by individuals to initiate action as prime movers, or by prime mover action within the several levels of educational governance if we are to restore our schools to be revalued as "a pearl of great price."

We will pay an even greater price
if we do not reclaim our schools.

End Notes

Chapter 1

[1]Ira Polley, "What's Right with our Education" (*Phi Delta Kappan*, September, 1969), p. 45.

[2]William J. Bennett. *Our Children and Our Country*. New York: Simon and Schuster, 1988, pp. 9-10.

[3]William D. Gardner. *War Against the Family*. Toronto, CN: Stoddard, 1992, p. 227.

Chapter 2

[1]Robert H. Anderson, "Education and the Evolving National Purpose" (*Educational Leadership*, January, 1976), p. 250.

[2]Ralph W. Tyler, "Tomorrow's Education" (*American Education*, August-September, 1975).

[3]Georgie Anne Geyer. *Americans No More*. New York: The Atlantic Monthly Press, 1996.

[4]Newt Gingrich. *To Renew America*. New York: Harper Collins Publisher, 1995.

[5]E.D. Hirsch, Jr. *The Schools We Need*. New York: Doubleday, 1966, p. 16.

[6]Diane Ravitch. *The Schools We Deserve*. New York: Basic Books, Inc., 1985. p. 311.

[7]Thomas Sowell. *Inside American Education*. New York: The Free Press, 1993, p. 303.

Chapter 3

[1]Thomas Sowell. *Inside American Education*. New York: The Free Press, 1993, pp. 70-99.

[2]Chester E. Finn, Jr. *We Must Take Charge*. New York: The Free Press, 1991, p. 263.

Chapter 4

[1]Gene Owens, "Editorial" (Mobile, AL: *Mobile Register*, November 7, 1997).

[2]William J. Bennett, "The Index of Leading Cultural Indicators, Vol. 1" (The Heritage Foundation, March, 1993).

[3]Martin L. Gross. *The End of Sanity*. New York: Avon Books, 1997, pp. 1-3, 31-33, 36-37.

[4]Angelo M. Codevilla. *The Character of Nations*. New York: Harper Collins, 1997, p. 284.

[5]Barbara Reynolds, "Without You Graduates, We Don't Have A Prayer," *USA Today*, June 25, 1993.

[6]Quotation from Chief Justice Rehquist's dissent in Wallace v. Jaffree, 472 U.S. 38 (1985), in which the Supreme Court invalidated a law to permit a moment of silence at public schools, because it expressly permitted silent prayer.

[7]Lino Graglia, "Editorial" (*National Review*, August 14, 1995).

[8]J. M. O'Neil. *Religion and Education under the Constitution*, 5th Ed. New York: Da Capo, 1972, p. 63.

[9]bid., pp. 219-233.

Chapter 5

[1]John E. Chubb and Terry M. Moe. *Politics, Markets and America's School*. Washington, DC: The Brookings Institute, 1990, p. 193.

[2] Thomas Sowell, *Inside American Education*. New York: The Free Press, 1993, p. 11.

[3]Chester E. Finn, Jr. *We Must Take Charge*. New York: The Free Press, 1991, p. 44.

[4]E. D. Hirsch, Jr. *The Schools We Need*. New York: Doubleday, 1996, pp 4, 69-126.

[5]Ibid, p 230

[6]Marvin Cetron and Margaret Gayle. *Education Renaissance*. New York: St. Martin's Press, 1991, p. 49.

[7]Madeline Hunter. *Teach More Faster*. El Segundo, CA:

Tip Publications, 1969.

Chapter 6
[1]Robert H. Bork. *Slouching Towards Gomorrah*. New York: Harper Collins, 1996, p. 25.

[2]Chester E. Finn, Jr. *We Must Take Charge*. New York: The Free Press, 1991, p. 195.

[3]Edward B. Fiske. *Smart Schools, Smart Kids*. New York: Simon and Schuster, 1991, pp. 258-259.

[4]Diane Ravitch. *The Schools We Deserve*. New York: Basic Books, Inc., 1985 pp. 91-92.

Chapter 7
[1]Robert S. Soar, Donald M. Medley and Homer Coker, "Teacher Evaluation: A Critique of Currently Used Methods" (*Phi Delta Kappan*, December 1983), pp. 239-246.

[2]Marvin Cetron and Margaret Gayle. *Educational Renaissance*. New York: St. Martin's Press, 1991, p. 135.

Chapter 8
[1]Edward B. Fiske. *Smart Schools, Smart Kids*. New York: Simon and Schuster, 1991, p. 166.

[2]James Patterson and Peter Kim. *The Second American Revolution*. New York: William Morrow and Company, Inc., 1994, p. 114.

[3]Chester E. Finn, Jr. *We Must Take Charge*. New York: The Free Press, 1991, p. 64.

[4]Edward B. Fiske. *Smart Schools, Smart Kids*. New York: Simon and Schuster, 1991, p. 199.

[5]John E. Chubb and Terry M. Moe. *Politics, Markets and American Schools*. Washington, DC: The Brookings Institute, 1990, p. 218.

[6]Ibid., p. 217.

Chapter 9

[1]Amy Stuart Wells. *Time To Choose*. New York: Hill and Wang, 1953, p. 96.

[2]E. D. Hirsch, Jr. *The Schools We Need*. New York: Doubleday, 1996, p. 62.

[3]Ted Kolderie, "The Charter Schools Idea," *Public Services Redesign Project* (St. Paul: Center for Policy Studies, June 18, 1992).

[4]Thomas Toch, "The New Education Bazaar" (*U.S. News and World Report*, April 27, 1998).

Chapter 10

[1]Chester E. Finn. *We Must Take Charge*. New York: The Free Press, 1991, p. 159.

[2]Edys S. Quellmalz, "Needed: Better Methods for Testing Higher-Order Thinking Skills," *Educational Leadership*, October, 1985.

[3]E. D. Hirsch Jr. *The Schools We Need*. New York: Doubleday, 1996, p. 177.

[4]Thomas Toch, "The New Education Bazaar" (*U.S. News and World Report*, April, 1996), p. 35.

[5]John E. Chubb and Terry M. Moe. *Politics, Markets and American Schools*. Washington, DC: The Brookings Institute, 1990, p. 198.

[6]Amy Stuart Wells. *Time to Choose*. New York: Hill and Wang, 1993, pp. 192-193.

Chapter 11

[1]John Rydor, "Mainstreaming" (*Today's Education*, March-April, 1976), p. 5.

[2]Jill Bloom. *Parenting Our Schools*. Boston: Little, Brown and Company, 1992, p. 210.

[3]Seymour B. Sarason. *The Predictable Failure of Educational Reform*. San Francisco: Jossey-Bass Publishers, 1990, pp. 28-29.

[4]George F. Will, "Healthy Inequality" (*Newsweek*, October 28, 1996).

[5]Ernest L. Boyer, "Public Law 94-142: A Promising Start?" (*Educational Leadership*, 1979), pp. 298-301.

Chapter 12

[1]David Harman. *Illiteracy, A National Dilemma.* New York: Cambridge Press, 1987, pp. 47-60.

[2]Samuel Blumenfeld, "The Victims of Dick and Jane" (*American Education*, 1982).

[3]Ibid.

[4]E. D. Hirsch, Jr. *The Schools We Need.* New York: Doubleday, 1996, p 221.

[5]Charles J. Sykes. *Dumbing Down Our Kids.* New York: St. Martins Press, 1995, p. 110.

[6]Blumenfed, op cit.

Chapter 13

[1]Robert G. Canfield, "How Useful Are Lessons on Listening?" (*Elementary School Journal*, December 1961), pp. 147-151.

[2]Frank B. May, "The Effects of Environment on Oral Language Development" (*Elementary English*, 43: November, 1966), pp. 720-729.

[3]Ruth G. Strickland. *The Language Arts in the Elementary School, 3rd Ed.* Lexington, MA: D. C. Heath and Company, 1969.

Chapter 14

[1]Seymour B. Sarason. *The Predictable Failure of Educational Reform.* San Francisco: Jossey-Bass, Inc., 1990, p. 50.

[2]John E. Chubb and Terry M. Moe. *Politics, Markets and America's Schools.* Washington, DC: The Brookings Institute, 1990, p. 49.

[3]Jill Bloom. *Parenting Our Schools.* Boston: Little,

Brown and Company, 1992, p. 142.

[4]Bill Honig. *Last Chance for Our Children*. Reading, MA: Addison Wesley Publishing Company, Inc., 1985, p. 159.

[5]Ibid.

[6]Jill Bloom, op cit., p. 128.

[7]Honig, op cit., p. 160.

Chapter 15

[1]Bill Honig. <u>Last Chance for Our Children</u>. Reading, MA: Addison-Wesley Publishing Company, 1985, p.. 135.

[2]Jill Bloom. *Parenting Our Schools*. Boston: Little, Brown and Company, Inc., 1992, p. 9.

[3]"Search of Students," <u>New Jersey v. T.L.O.</u>, *Supreme Court Decision*, January 15, 1935.

[4]Morrel J. Clute, "Rights and Responsibilities of Students" (*Educational Leadership*, December, 1968), pp. 240-242.

[5]Honig, op cit., p. 136.

[6]Ibid., p. 130.

Chapter 16

[1]Allen Small, "What's Wrong with the P.T.A.?" (*Phi Delta Kappan*, June, 1964), p. 456.

[2]Melitta Cutright. *The National P.T.A. Talks to Parents*. New York: Doubleday, 1944.

[3]Jill Bloom. *Parenting Our Schools*. Boston: Little, Brown and Company, Inc., 1992, p. 19.

[4]Ibid., p. 8.

Chapter 17

[1]Daniel C. Neale, "A Matter of Shaping" (*Phi Delta Kappan*, March, 1966), p. 375.

[2]John E. Cooper, "The Nature and Purpose of Discipline" (The National Education Association, *Discipline and Learning*, 1975), p. 11.

Chapter 18

[1]Bill Honig. *Last Chance for Our Schools*. Reading, MA: Addison-Wesley Publishing Company, Inc., 1985, p. 139

Chapter 19

[1]Jill Bloom. *Parenting Our Schools*. Boston: Little, Brown and Company, 1992, pp. 201-202.
[2]Newt Gingrich. *To Renew America*. New York: Harper Collins, 1995, pp. 161-162.
[3]Martin Gross. *The End of Sanity*. New York: Avon Books, 1997, pp. 172-173.
[4]Bill Honig. *Last Chance for Our Children*. Reading, MA: Addison-Wesley Publishing Company, Inc., 1985, pp. 77-78.

Chapter 20

[1]Thomas E. Gatewood, "What Research Says about the Middle School" (*Eduational Leadership*, December, 1973), p. 222.
[2]Alvin W. Howard. *Teaching in the Middle Schools*. Scranton, PA: International Textbook Company, 1968, p. 11.
[3]Sidney P. Rollins, "Youth Education Problems" (ASCD, National Education Association, *Youth Education*, 1968), pp. 5-19.
[4]Donald H. Eichorn, "The Nature of Transescents" from *Perspectives, Middle School Education*. Macon, GA: Pana Print, 1984, pp. 30-31.
[5]Ibid.
[6]William M. Alexander and Emmett L. Williams, "Schools for the Middle Years" (Educational Leadership, December, 1965), p. 217.
[7]Mary F. Compton, "How Do You Prepare to Teach Transescent *Educational Leadership*, December, 1973), p. 214.

[8]John H. Wonsbury and Gordon E. Varr. *A Curriculum for the Middle School Years*. New York: Harper and Row Publishers, 1978, p. 12.

Chapter 21

[1]Gail McCutcheon, "The Curriculum:Patchwork or Crazy Quilt? (*Educational Leadership*, 30:2, November 1978), p. 114.
[2]Jonathan Yardley, "Editorial" (*The Washington Post*, April 3, 1994).
[3]Jerome S. Bruner. *Toward a Theory of Instruction*. Cambridge, MA: Harvard University Press, 1966, p. 44.
[4]Martha Woodall, "Editorial" (*Knight-Ridder Newspapers*, November 5, 1995).

Chapter 22

[1]Diane Ravitch. *The Schools We Deserve*. New York: Basic Books, Inc., 1985, pp. 47-49.
[2]Bill Honig. *Last Chance for Our Children*. Reading, MA: Addison-Wesley Publishing Company, Inc., 1985, p. 50.

Chapter 23

[1]Armin Paul Thies, "Neuropsychological Approaches to Learning Disorders" (American Education Research Association, *Review of Research in Education*, 1985, pp. 95, 102.
[2]Anne Marshall Huston. *Understanding Dyslexia, A Practical Approach for Parents and Teachers*. New York: Madison Books, 1992, p. 95.
[3]Lori and Bill Grainger. *The Magic Feather*: The *Truth About Special Education*. New York: E. D. Dutton, 1986, p. 165.

Chapter 24

[1]Gene I. Maeroff. *Don't Blame the Kids*. New York: McGraw-Hill Book Company, 1982, pp. 8-9.

[2]Ibid., p. 8.

[3]Diane Ravitch. . *The Schools We Deserve*. New York: Basic Books, Inc., 1985, p. 153.

[4]Thomas A. Shannon, "The Emerging Roles of the Federal Government in Public Education" (*Phi Delta Kappan*, 1982), p 595.

Chapter 25

[1]Henry Grady Weaver. *The Mainspring of Human Progress*. New York: The Foundation for Economic Education, 1947.

Chapter 26

[1]Dan Kubiak, "Political Power and the Schools—At the State Level" (*Educational Leadership*, October, 1970), p. 30.

[2]Diane Ravitch. *The Schools We Deserve*. New York: Basic Books, Inc., 1985, p. 92.

Chapter 27

[1]James Patterson and Peter Kim. *The Second American Revolution*. New York: William Morrow and Company, Inc., 1994, p. 18.

[2]John E. Chubb and Terry M. Moe. *Politics, Markets and America's Schools*. Washington, DC: The Brookings Institute, 1990, p. 5.

Chapter 28

[1]Samuel B. Bacharach. *Education Reforms, Making Sense of it All*. Boston: Allyn and Bacon, 1990, pp. 15, 70.

Chapter 29

[1]E. D. Hirsch, Jr. *The Schools We Need*. New York: Doubleday, 1966, p. 288.

[2]James Patterson and Peter Kim. *The Second American*

Revolution. New York: William Morrow and Company, Inc., 1994, p. 107.

Chapter 30

[1]Gene I. Maeroff. *Don't Blame the Kids*. New York: McGraw-Hill Book Company, 1982, p. 213.

[2]D. P. Crandall, J. W. Eiseman and K. S. Louis, (*Educational Administration Quarterly*, 22:3) pp. 21-53.

[3]Donald G. Nugent, "Are Local Control and Lay Boards Obsolete?" (*Educational Leadership* 22:2, November, 1964), p. 85.

[4]D. L. Clarke, L. S. Lotto and T. A. Astuto. "Effective Schools and School Improvement: A Comparative Analysis of Two Lines of Inquiry" (*Education Administration Quarterly* 20:3, 1984), p. 55

[5]Chester E. Finn, Jr., "A Call for Quality Education" (Time, Inc., *American Renewal*, 1981)

Chapter 31

[1]John E. Chubb and Terry M. Moe. *Politics, Markets and America's Schools*. Washington, DC: The Brookings Institute, 1990, p. 30.

[2]Charles J. Sykes. *Dumbing Down Our Kids*. New York: St. Martins Press, 1995, pp. 271-272.

[3]James K. Kent, "The Coleman Report: Opening Pandora's Box" (*Phi Delta Kappan*, January, 1968), p. 242.

[4]Glen E. Robinson, "Effective Schools Research: A Guide to School Improvement," *Educational Research Service*, February, 1985.

[5]Alexis Carrel. *Man the Unknown*. New York: Harper & Brothers, 1935, p. 141.

INDEX